Praise for *God in Translation*

Doreen M. McFarlane's *God in Translation: The Theological Gifts of Exploring Biblical Languages* offers a refreshing and accessible exploration of biblical texts that opens new windows for understanding God's nature through careful examination of Hebrew language and concepts, making complex theological ideas approachable for lay readers. Rather than claiming definitive answers, the book thoughtfully presents alternative possibilities for biblical interpretation—from nonhierarchical relationships to divine repentance—inviting readers to consider fresh perspectives that may deepen their faith and relationship with the divine. This engaging work successfully bridges scholarly biblical language study with practical application, providing both pastors and congregants with valuable tools for ongoing biblical research and spiritual growth.

—**Ananda Geyser-Fouché**, professor of Old Testament studies and Hebrew Scriptures, University of Pretoria; coeditor of *Emerging Sectarianism in the Dead Sea Scrolls: Continuity, Separation, and Conflict* and *Scribal Practice, Text and Canon in the Dead Sea Scrolls: Essays in Memory of Peter W. Flint*

God in Translation is a truly thought-provoking work that dares to explore fresh interpretations of Scripture, inviting readers to reconsider long-held assumptions about God's nature and our relationship with the divine. By delving into the nuances of biblical translation and posing insightful questions, this book opens exciting new avenues for understanding core theological concepts like hierarchy, disagreement, and even God's capacity for repentance. It's a valuable resource for anyone seeking a deeper, more expansive, and ultimately more relevant connection to biblical texts and their implications for our lives and faith communities.

—**Adam Snook**, assistant to the bishop, Eastern Synod, Evangelical Lutheran Church in Canada

Doreen M. McFarlane makes a passionate case for the study of biblical languages and translation, and for the relevance of that study for the church and its theologies. At a time when the future of theological scholarship and even higher education is uncertain, McFarlane's call for greater learning in communities of faith is a welcome contribution.

—**Ken Stone**, Distinguished Service Professor and professor of Bible, culture, and hermeneutics, Chicago Theological Seminary

This book is a rare find: a mix of cutting-edge biblical scholarship and relatable examples that reveal why understanding the original Hebrew text is so critically important for our lives today. *God in Translation* will make you rethink some of the Bible's most familiar stories. Doing so is not a mere academic exercise but, rather, opens new and exciting possibilities for engaging life's greatest questions and most important challenges.

—**Martha Tatarnic**, co-rector, St. George's Anglican Church, St. Catharines, Ontario

GOD IN TRANSLATION

GOD IN TRANSLATION

The Theological Gifts of Exploring Biblical Languages

Doreen M. McFarlane

FORTRESS PRESS
MINNEAPOLIS

GOD IN TRANSLATION
The Theological Gifts of Exploring Biblical Languages

30 29 28 27 26 25 1 2 3 4 5 6 7 8 9

Library of Congress Cataloging-in-Publication Data

Names: McFarlane, Doreen M. author
Title: God in translation : the theological gifts of exploring biblical languages / Doreen M. McFarlane.
Description: Minneapolis : Fortress Press, [2025] | Includes appendix. | Includes bibliographical references and index. |
Identifiers: LCCN 2025021674 (print) | LCCN 2025021675 (ebook) | ISBN 9798889834403 paperback | ISBN 9798889834410 ebook
Subjects: LCSH: God--Biblical teaching | Bible--Criticism, interpretation, etc.
Classification: LCC BS544 .M35 2025 (print) | LCC BS544 (ebook)
LC record available at https://lccn.loc.gov/2025021674
LC ebook record available at https://lccn.loc.gov/2025021675

Cover image: Compilation of stock textures from Getty Images
Cover design: Kris E. Miller

Print ISBN: 979-8-8898-3440-3
eBook ISBN: 979-8-8898-3441-0

This book is dedicated to my superb professors who taught at the Lutheran School of Theology at Chicago. Many of them had come out of the Concordia Seminary in Exile (Seminex), which existed from 1974 until 1987, when they moved to Chicago to teach. I am grateful for their courage in standing up for their principles in the face of fundamentalism, and for the exceptional biblical knowledge they passed on to their students in Chicago once they joined the LSTC teaching staff.

Contents

	Acknowledgments	ix
	Abbreviations	xi
	Bible Translations Mentioned in This Book	xiii
	Introduction	1
1.	Hierarchy	15
2.	Disagreement	29
3.	Repentance	43
4.	Enemies	51
5.	Love	61
6.	Wholeness	71
7.	Resurrection	79
8.	Embodiment	85
9.	Emotions	109
10.	Work/Worship	115
11.	Names of God	123
12.	Creation	133

13. The Good News 141

Appendix: Study Resources 147

Bibliography 159

Index 165

Acknowledgments

I am particularly grateful to Fortress Press editor-in-chief Laura Gifford. She has shepherded me all the way through, from initial meetings with committees who asked questions and added excellent suggestions as the book took shape, right up to the final edits. Laura offers insight, efficiency, and kindness, all of which have made the hard work in creating and publishing this book both exciting and satisfying. She has taken the time to be sure this book is the best it can be. Thank you, Laura, and those on your staff who were involved, from the bottom of my heart.

I also want to thank my husband, Eigil. In this, our first year of marriage, he has spent much time affording me the quiet and space that was needed, along with suggestions and encouragement at every step along the way.

Abbreviations

BDB — *The Brown-Driver-Briggs Hebrew and English Lexicon*
JBL — *Journal of Biblical Literature*
LXX — Septuagint (Greek Old Testament / Prime Testament)
OED — *Oxford English Dictionary*
TDOT — *Theological Dictionary of the Old Testament*

Bible Translations Mentioned in This Book

ASV	—	American Standard Version
CEB	—	Common English Bible
EASY	—	EasyEnglish Bible
ESV	—	English Standard Version
GNT-CE	—	Good News Translation, Catholic Edition
GNT	—	Good News Translation. Also known as the Good News Bible (GNB).
GW	—	GOD'S WORD Translation
JB	—	Jerusalem Bible
JPS Tanakh	—	1917—Jewish Publication Society (includes the Torah, the Prophets, and Writings).
KJV	—	King James Version
LB	—	Living Bible. Also known as The Living Bible (TLB).
MEV	—	Modern English Version
MSG	—	The Message
NAB	—	New American Bible
NASB	—	New American Standard Bible
NIRV	—	New International Reader's Version
NIV	—	New International Version
NJB	—	New Jerusalem Bible
NKJV	—	New King James Version
NLT	—	New Living Translation
NRSV	—	New Revised Standard Version

NRSVCE	—	New Revised Standard Version, Catholic Edition
NRSVue	—	New Revised Standard Version, Updated Edition
RNJB	—	Revised New Jerusalem Bible
RSV	—	Revised Standard Version
VOICE	—	The Voice
WYC	—	Wycliffe Bible. Also known as the Middle English Bible (MEB).

Introduction

How much do we really know about God, God's nature, and God's behavior? How much *can* we know? Over centuries, God has too often been perceived as some kind of elderly "man in the sky," and too often as one who is demanding, wrathful, and angry. What can we discover if we are willing to dig deeper into the biblical texts and the biblical languages? In this twenty-first century, our congregations and religious leaders consist of intelligent people who can be excited and curious about the Bible's messages when these messages are offered to them with new and engaging possibilities to consider. Exploring theological topics through a lexical lens can present opportunities to investigate what is written in the biblical texts about the nature of God, as well as about our relationships with God and each other. Throughout the pages of this book, we will explore exciting and sometimes even startling possibilities about the nature of God as presented in the Hebrew Bible / Old Testament.[1] These attributes and behaviors are often missed when we engage only with the traditionally accepted and sometimes incomplete, or even inaccurate, translations of the Bible. When taking the time to

1 In this first volume, references will be from Hebrew scripture (Old Testament). The nature and behavior of God as known in the New Testament will be reserved for another volume.

consider alternative translations, we encounter texts that focus on God in ways that can alter or even change our understandings, our attitudes, and our lives for the better.

ABOUT GOD AND ABOUT US

This book asks questions and ponders possible answers to a wide variety of questions we may never have asked about God. Before we begin analyzing biblical texts directly, we will consider some of the issues that tend to make biblical translation difficult or at least challenging. Chapter one, "Hierarchy," asks the following questions: "What if the God of the Bible really is nonhierarchical?" "What if this means women and men are truly equal?" "What if men came to realize they were not responsible for everything, and what if women had never felt put down or unequal?" "What if woman is, and has always been, intended to be much more than an assistant or a helper to man, but rather an equal partner and strong advocate?" In chapter two, "Disagreement," we look at the question "What if God doesn't expect us to always acquiesce, and is pleased if, at appropriate times, we are willing to stand up to God and even to argue?" What if, in the past—in Job, for example—we have interpreted the book to fit our preconceived notions and lost track of the even better news the book contains in doing so? Next, in chapter three, "Repentance," we ponder the question "What if God is willing to recognize God's own mistakes or wrong intentions, say 'I'm sorry,' and repent and change?" How would that affect our own ability to see things that we have done or thought wrong and to apologize to God and to each other? In chapter four, "Enemies," we ask, "If God is not against our enemies, might we treat them differently?" and "What if we could recognize at times that others were doing the best they could?" Delving even more deeply into the texts, we will consider the possibility that God, as known in the Bible, may not have the same attitude as we do in relation to our enemies or even to God's enemies. In chapter five, "Love," we will search for what we can learn about the real meaning (or meanings) of God's love in scripture. We will ask how a better understanding of this love might affect our relationships with God and with each other. What if we could begin to learn to love the ways God loves: freely and magnanimously? In chapter six, "Wholeness," we ask, "What if God sees each of us as undivided and we could envision ourselves less as being compartmentalized and composed of separate parts (e.g., body, soul, and spirit) but rather as one being, and whole?" In conjunction with this, chapter seven, "Resurrection," asks, "What has God really promised us about the resurrection of the body and the afterlife?" and "What can the Bible tell us about heaven, if anything?" Chapter eight, "Embodiment," will address questions such as the following: "God is pure spirit, but was it ever believed, in biblical times, that God had a physical body?" "Was that body perceived as male or female?" "How might we view God differently if God is seen as having masculine traits, attributes, and behaviors?" "And what about those who may have considered God as inhabiting female aspects?" In chapter nine, "Emotions," we will consider the use of the words "jealous" and "zealous," which have been used interchangeably regarding God but which, in English, have quite different meanings. We will ask, "Is God jealous?" and "Is God zealous?" In chapter ten, "Work/Worship," we ask, "What does it mean that while God intended us to work, it is often clear that our work needs to be a joy, and a privilege?" We learn that one main Hebrew word for work (*avodah*) means "labor" but also means both "service" and "worship." The history of work in this world has been one that included much suffering. We ask, "Might we have perceived our work differently if we had known work in the Bible can also mean 'worship' and 'service'?" Chapter eleven, "Names of God," will discuss the variety of monikers that have been given to God in the Bible and addresses the following questions: "Can we know God's name?" "Does God even have a name?" "How have mistranslations complicated our understanding of God's name and nature?" "Are we permitted to know and speak God's name?" "How does knowing God's name, or not knowing it, affect our relationship with God?" Chapter twelve, "Creation," addresses the fact that, in Hebrew, there is a word used solely for the work of creating in which God engages. This word is never used to describe the work, or what we would call, in English, "creative work" that is done by humans. In chapter thirteen, "The Good News," all these biblical actions and attributes of God and their consequences for us are summed up. An addendum follows, which offers a plan of action for readers to move forward, engaging on their own or with others with similar interests, in this type of biblical study. One format will be offered for those with a knowledge of Biblical Hebrew and Greek, and a second one for those without these language skills, who can proceed from whatever level is comfortable for them.

The volume concludes with an argument for studying the Biblical languages, including the wise comments of Martin Luther on this topic.

Whether or not readers choose to move forward with their own research, the biblical translation treasures in this book will present readers with new and more expansive ways of understanding biblical texts and communicating with God as known in the Bible. This should lead to the possibility of new insights into preaching or responding to sermons, and leading and participating in Bible study, as well as prayer and personal reflection. These eye-opening options for translations will present a glimpse into the joy and importance of connecting with the Biblical languages.

In these often difficult and challenging times in which we are living there is a renewed hunger for better understanding of our faith and for understanding God. Many people possess a sincere yearning to know God better but do not know where to begin. People long for good news in these sometimes-confusing days and are eager to learn more. And pastors, you can trust your congregation's eager willingness to learn more, as well as their good judgment when they are given the opportunity to grow in understanding about God and their faith! When everybody learns, everybody wins. I hope this book will bring joy and renewed life to preaching and biblical study, to the life of the church, and to personal lives.

ABOUT TRANSLATION

Overview of Currently Popular Translations

Good biblical translations are vitally important to understanding scripture, but churchgoers are too often accustomed to simply accepting the translations in their own language that have been presented to them by their religious institutions. Most people have not given any thought to the fact that their Bibles were, of course, written by a wide variety of ancient people, in ancient languages, and in ancient times that are very different from our own. There is nothing particularly wrong with these translations. The clergy and clerical hierarchy who chose them intended, of course, to offer the best. They, like all the rest of us, however, have both deliberate and unintentional biases that have affected these choices. Some are related to the doctrine of a particular denomination. Others, however, may emanate from issues related to power.[2] Specific translations have been given the stamp of approval within certain denominations. Other denominations have chosen to keep the options open to their people but tend to favor specific versions in the context of liturgy and worship. For example, until 1979 the Roman Catholic Church only accepted the Clementine Vulgate of 1598 (the Latin translation of the Bible). It now approves of the NRSVCE, the JB and RNJB, the GNT, the GNT-CE, the NAB, and the pre–King James Douay-Rheims Bible of 1582. Southern Baptists, on the other hand, do not dictate which Bible versions their adherents may use. Still, they give deference to the KJV, NKJV, and the NIV. Methodists tend to prefer the NIV and the NRSV. ELCA Lutherans in general prefer the NRSV or its updated edition (NRSVue), while Missouri Synod Lutherans have chosen the ESV as their official translation. Many Pentecostals prefer the KJV. These Bibles, of course, are all translating (into English, in

2 Doreen M. McFarlane, "How Biblical Translation Choices Forward Clergy Power and Control," lecture delivered at the Bible in America section of the Society of Biblical Literature Annual Meeting, San Diego, CA, November 25, 2024.

our case) the same texts (from Hebrew, Greek, and some Aramaic). For this reason, it is enlightening to read and compare.

All this said, not too many churchgoers have given much thought to the translations they and their clergy are using, nor have they taken the opportunity of comparing the many and various versions. In many churches, though scripture is recited from the pulpit and lectern, no Bibles at all are in the pews. Still, many people today, if given the chance, would be willing to set aside older concepts and look at what knowledge might be gleaned directly from the biblical text. This is especially useful in the vital matter of understanding the nature of God as God is known through the words of the Bible. Alternate translations can present exceptionally good news, new ideas to consider, and opportunities for growth for those who are willing to take a fresh look at these very ancient texts.

Because all the copies of the original texts of the Bible are essentially the same, most people, it seems, are scarcely aware of what might be called any "agenda" behind the decisions, intentional and unintentional, that have been made by the translators in the version of the Bible they are employing. A detailed discussion is, of course, beyond the scope of this volume, but resources are available to get a general overview regarding the many versions.[3] Below are just a few examples of how the same texts can be translated in different ways when there are different agendas and different translators. Such translators might, for example, be liberal or conservative, female or male, and coming from varying cultural backgrounds, as well as being older or younger.

The KJV was commissioned in the year 1604 and published by the Church of England in 1611 under the sponsorship of King James I/VI. This translation is known to be archaic, but also poetic and beautiful. Until recent decades, the KJV was so beloved that many people would be offended if they were required to hear or recite any more up-to-date version. This was likely because the words

3 See *A User's Guide to Bible Translations: Making the Most of Different Versions*, by David Dewey (Downers Grove, IL: InterVarsity Press, 2004).

they had read and prayed and memorized as children had become deeply fixed in their minds and hearts. This had been the case in the English language for over four hundred years. In the meantime, English grammar and the language itself were dramatically changing. Now, even though most people can still pretty much discern and appreciate the KJV's version of English, they have come to be more interested in being able to understand the meaning of the texts. The newer versions, for example, have dropped the words *thee* and *thou*, and employ common words such as *you*. Psalm 23 offers a good example of how the language has changed from version to version. Choice of language in the KJV tends to be patriarchal, and this has been adapted as needed in more modern versions. For example, when the word *sons* indicates both sons and daughters, that language will often be changed to say *children* or *sons and daughters*. Probably one of the most appropriate word changes is from *man* and *mankind* to *human* and *humankind*, indicating all people. The KJV is still treasured, while, for deeper understanding, some other versions may prove more useful, especially to younger people who do not recognize the archaic language. More sadly, many magnificent religious musical works such as oratorios and other English-language church music, written by famous composers of the past and employing King James texts for lyrics, are now, unfortunately, too often being forfeited.

The RSV was produced with wide denominational support in 1952. For its time, it was a big change for the better. It offered a more accurate and faithful translation of the original scriptures. It was also more readable, employing contemporary language. It was followed by the NRSV in 1990, taking into account the discoveries of the Dead Sea Scrolls and other documents. Its objective was to improve paragraphs and punctuation, to eliminate archaic language, to improve accuracy and clarity, and to eliminate masculine oriented language (except for God).[4] The NRSVue, as of 2022, attempts to remove gender bias and to provide additional clarity, as well as to

---

4 Dewey, *Bible Translations*, 170.

bring greater precision in consideration of new textual evidence, historical insights and philological understandings.[5]

A few other important translations include the JB, the LB, and the NIV, all of which have been and remain popular choices. The JB was published in 1966 and revised to the NJB in 1985. It was translated from the French, and the translators made an attempt to have words remain consistent throughout. The New Testament of the NIV was published in 1973 and the full version in October of 1978. By the late 1980s, the NIV outsold the KJV and became the most popular Bible for general readership. As of March 2022, the NIV remained number one. But the NLT, a paraphrase of the Bible designed for readability and published in 1996, had moved from number four to number two in popularity. The KJV had shifted from number two to number four.

Regardless of the version of the Bible that is employed, the Bible still presents many difficulties in translating and understanding. To begin, the Old Testament / First Testament / Prime Testament, or Hebrew Bible, was composed over centuries by many people in ancient times and in ancient Hebrew (with some Aramaic), and the New Testament in a Biblical Greek known as *koine*. Some books of the Bible have multiple authors. We know this from the style of writing, as the actual authors are unknown. Some passages in both Testaments are written in the simple, straightforward language of the people (e.g., Jonah and Ruth). Other portions are written in what appears to be highly academic or stylized language (e.g., Job, Song of Songs, and Isaiah). We do not know who wrote the biblical books, even though names have been assigned to them. (To title a writing in honor and memory of another person, often a long-deceased person of high regard, was the norm.)

To add to the difficulty, no less than one third of the Old Testament is written in poetry. Ancient Hebrew poetic rules and style clearly are very different from those of English, and we do not know at all what those rules were. We can only guess. Sometimes we can discern a style. Here are a few examples from the NRSVue:

5 Dewey, *Bible Translations*, 170.

Psalm 51:10–11—"Create in me a clean heart, O God" matches with the next line, "And put a new and right spirit within me." To create a clean heart in the person is like putting a right spirit in the person. Then, the text says, "Do not cast me away from your presence," followed by another matching phrase, "and do not take your holy spirit from me." To not cast one away is a similar or matching phrase to not taking God's holy spirit out of the person.

Psalm 83:1—"O God, do not keep silent" and "Do not hold your peace or be still, O God!" In this example, "do not keep silent" matches in meaning with "do not hold your peace."

Psalm 95:1—"O come, let us sing to the Lord. Let us make a joyful noise to the rock of our salvation." Note here that "let us sing" matches with "Let us make a joyful noise." Further, "the Lord" matches with the description of God as "the rock of our salvation."

There are hundreds of such examples of poetry in the Bible. It has been suggested by biblical scholars that presenting two separate but similar ideas shows readers they can never determine fundamentally the absolute will of God. Rather, speaking from a more spiritual point of view, one could say that the matching poetic phrases give the Holy Spirit space to breathe through and between the lines of text.

As mentioned above, we do not know the rules of ancient Hebrew poetry. Translators from Hebrew into English have even sometimes tried to make the words fit into something like an English-language type of poetry. Others have kept their translations as close as possible to what they believed the text to mean literally, even though the original intent may never have been for it to have been taken literally. In addition, syntax (word order) varies widely from language to language. In Hebrew, the normal order would generally be verb, subject, object. When translators change the order to fit our English-language expectations, much literary artistry can be lost.[6] Meaning can also

6 Robert Alter, *The Art of Bible Translation* (Princeton, NJ: Princeton University Press, 2019), 56.

most certainly be lost. In addition, sound play and wordplay, when altered, can cause us to easily lose the mood of the ancient text or even misunderstand its intention completely.

A clear example of Hebrew syntax is found at Genesis 1:12—וַתּוֹצֵא הָאָרֶץ דֶּשֶׁא—which literally means "and brought forth the earth grass." In English, of course, it would read "and the earth brought forth grass."

Copies of the biblical text from ancient times were remarkably accurate and consistent, considering all the things that could have gone wrong in copying. First, as we know, there was no such thing as a printing press until Johannes Gutenberg began designing his invention around 1436.[7] Before that date, all Bibles were therefore hand copied by scribes. There could have been, and probably were, many reasons for changes or mistakes in copying. In medieval monasteries, for example, scribes spent their lives copying biblical and other texts. They generally worked together in a large room known as a scriptorium (the Latin word for a place of writing). Some scribes would be positioned up front, but others toward the rear of the room. The light in such a room would change throughout the course of the day, and as the daylight faded, at times become quite dim. The scribes tended to maintain their jobs as they aged, so it was possible a scribe might, over the years, have become quite hard of hearing, and he might well have been positioned in the back of the room. As he listened to someone a fair distance from him reciting the text for copying, it would have been easy to misunderstand what was being spoken aloud and to copy it incorrectly. A scribe could, on the other hand, have acquired sight impediments and might easily make mistakes in what he was writing. In addition, it has been suggested that even scribes who were accurately copying from one text onto another might have disagreed with the text in front of them at times and made the independent decision to adjust a text to supposedly "correct" what had been written, assuming that the earlier copy contained a mistake.

---

7 Woodblock printing, however, was invented in China in the 9th century!

Perhaps the most treacherous issue for us in understanding the meaning of a text, however, remains in translation and in word choice. There are, as we know in English, many ways that one thing can be said, and there can also be great nuance among these word choices. Every time a word is chosen for a Bible translation, an interpretive decision is being made. In the case of many biblical translations in modern times, these choices are determined by committees and groups who have been given the responsibility (and the power) to choose what a word means in context. On the other hand, in some cases, there are entire translations made by one individual.[8] The reader would have to determine whether that person was qualified to make these kinds of decisions. We must also remember that there are up to thousands of years' distance between the time of the writings of the Bible and the time of the translations. It is almost impossible, however hard we study, for us to really comprehend the environment, lifestyle, and ways of thinking of these ancient people. Yet the Bible has still been passed down to us, and it deeply affects our lives.

To confuse matters further, there are words that only appear once in the Bible. These are known by scholars as *hapax legomena* (which means in Greek "once said"). There are 1,480 of these in the Bible, though only 400 are true *hapax legomena* because the rest are words with added roots, suffixes, and prefixes. Still, problems arise because, if a word appears in the Bible only once, there is no way to really know what it meant unless it appears in other related literature. One can only guess by its context.

Another issue, and one that will arise in this book, is that it appears the biblical writers were by no means averse to employing words that had varying meanings. And it was not at all uncommon for such words, in fact, even at times to have opposite meanings! An example would be the Hebrew word בָּרוּךְ (*baruch*). This word generally means "bless" but can sometimes infer a meaning of "curse." The

8 e.g., David Bentley Hart, trans., *The New Testament: A Translation* (New Haven, CT: Yale University Press, 2017); and Robert Alter, *The Hebrew Bible: A Translation with Commentary* (New York: W. W. Norton & Company, 2018).

word is related to going down on one's knees. Its use in the English translation of Job 2:9 is a good example. In the English translation, Job's wife says to him, "Curse God and die." But the word *baruch* properly and primarily means "bless." This would, at first, appear to be a translation mistake, but knowing the context in Job, it appears to be correct. Later, in Job 42, there is a sentence that can be translated in opposite ways (which will be discussed in detail in chapter three). Biblical Hebrew is a language that can be read in very different and sometimes even contradictory or opposite ways. This style of writing, rather than simply confusing the reader (and it often does so), also has a bright side. It offers readers the capacity to bring to the texts differing and even opposite meanings. This allows us to open our hearts and minds to many possibilities and, sometimes, to even change our minds in relation to concepts that may have quite convinced us, or to hold the two meanings in tension. This, too, will be discussed further in chapter three.

Format

In the core of this volume, each chapter will address specific questions about an attribute or behavior of God as known in scripture. Where appropriate, more "traditional" translations from versions such as the NKJV, NIV, NRSV, or NRSVue or related texts will be presented, along with alternate (equally accurate) translations that suggest attributes of God that we may not yet have considered. We will explore these through the lens of scholarship, including biblical commentaries, lexicons, study guides, dictionaries and concordances, consultation with rabbis, the Septuagint's translation of the Hebrew Bible into Greek, scholarly journals, and books. (The details of sources will be listed in footnotes.) Next, we will analyze the meanings of those translations that appear to be the most accurate and why. Following this, a short "scenario" or life story will be presented for each chapter, showing how this alternate understanding of the meaning of the text can impact very real lives and life situations.

Then, each chapter concludes with a section entitled "So, Therefore, What?" In this section, we will consider this different way of looking at God's attribute or behavior, asking how a new awareness of the text in this regard might make our own lives different or better, or change our behavior or attitude toward God and each other.

Now let us begin to analyze the behaviors and attributes of God as we can discern them from the Bible, and as we consider the various translations and possibilities that arise in relation to them. We are taught at the outset, of course, that God is good, and that God loves us and loves all people. But what gems in the biblical texts might have we missed in the past, especially about the nature and behavior of God? And in what ways can these move us forward to enhance our understanding of this most important of relationships?

CHAPTER 1

Hierarchy

THE QUESTION: WHAT IF GOD IS NONHIERARCHICAL?

Hierarchy, by the nature of the meaning of the word, infers a top-down list of powers and behaviors. How many of us were raised within hierarchical systems, believing the generally unspoken idea that the order of importance was pretty much this: God, Jesus, the Holy Spirit, man, woman, children, animals and birds, and then maybe snakes and crawling things? We have, of course, been taught in Christian doctrine that God is Three Persons in One: Father, Son, and Holy Spirit, or, using words more comfortable to some, Creator, Redeemer, and Sanctifier. Regarding the rest of the list, there is much in the biblical texts to suggest to us that God, although all-powerful, does not view the world this way at all. What would our world be like if we came to truly realize that women and men were always intended to be equal and to perceive each other as equals, working together for good, finding solace in each other, and having respect for each other and for all animal and plant life?[1] For example, in recent years, animal studies have emerged as a part of biblical studies programs.[2] Animals appear throughout the Bible from Genesis to Revelation.

---

1 It is of particular importance to understand this as the world faces serious climate change.

2 The Society of Biblical Literature now has an Animal Studies program unit.

Regarding the issue of humans, male and female, importantly we now are beginning to understand that many people do not identify specifically as male or female[3] and, of course, everyone is beloved by God. The scope of such a study means this matter will need to be addressed in other volumes, though we will see in chapter eight that God has been clearly described in the Bible in terms of both body parts and behaviors that are male, female, or beyond any binary categories.

Unfortunately, over too many generations, both males and females have been taught, in and out of church, that God expects women to be subservient and obedient to the men in their lives. But the question is, Does God in the Bible actually ever pronounce that men should control women or that women are inferior in any way? Or has the church too often just chosen to interpret the Bible that way? In what ways would our lives and our relationship with God be different if we understood that God has created women and men to be in equal partnership, or in relationship in ways different from what we had assumed?

LOOKING AT THE TEXTS

We can look to the creation stories in Genesis to see where the misunderstandings about the relationship between male and female begin, and search out a way to a clearer understanding of what that relationship was intended to be.

There are two different and distinct creation narratives in Genesis. At the earliest mention of the creation of humans in Genesis 1:26, there are at least three matters to be noted. Verse 26 says, "Then God said, 'Let us make humans [אָדָם (*adam*)] in our own image, according to our likeness.'" The word *adam* here is not the personal name Adam and rather appears to be without gender or androgenous (having characteristics of both male and female). It means something

3 These are LGBTQIA2S+.

akin to "earthling," as coming from the word אֲדָמָה (*adamah*), which means "ground" or "land" (Gen 2:5; 4:2; Exod 34:26). This would imply someone who was created from materials of the earth and not any kind of an angel or spirit. It also makes clear that God made this human not to be a god but still to be somehow like God, as the phrases "in our image" בְּצַלְמֵנוּ (*bezalmenu*) and "according to our likeness" דְמוּתֵנוּ (*demutenu*) are used here. It is typical of Hebrew poetry, as mentioned earlier, to describe something in two different ways consecutively. The beauty of this is that the reader is presented with two similar but not identical choices regarding the meaning, thereby allowing the spirit metaphorically to "breathe" between the two descriptions so the text allows for more than one interpretation. To be made "in our image" and "according to our likeness" may imply a mirror-like image, but it does not mean a direct copy. This human is then said to have been given dominion/rule over all the fish, birds, cattle, and creeping things on the earth. In verse 27b, humankind is mentioned again, but this time "in the image of God he created them; male and female he created them" (*him* in Hebrew). From there, they are blessed and given their duty to be fruitful and multiply, to fill the earth and subdue it, and to have dominion over fish, birds, and every living creature. It seems very clear from the above text that in no place is the male directed to wield power over the female.

Immediately following the above text, a second and separate creation story is presented, beginning at Genesis 2:4. This story more specifically gives the purpose of humans as being created to till the ground. Genesis 2:5b–7 says: "The Lord God [*Yahweh Elohim*] formed [hu]man [הָאָדָם (*adam*)[4]] from the dust [עָפָר (*afar*)[5]] of the ground [הָאֲדָמָה (*ha adam-ah*)[6]] and breathed into his nostrils the breath of life, and the [hu]man became a living being [נֶפֶשׁ חַיָּה (*nephesh ha-ya*)][7]." Following this, God plants a garden in Eden and places

4 Francis Brown, S. R. Driver, and Charles A. Briggs, BDB 9a.

5 BDB 68a.

6 BDB 9b.

7 BDB 659a, 224.

the human in the garden. Still, in this narrative, the human is not specified as male. God then creates all the other living things, and the human names them. God has promised a suitable partner, but none of the animals will apparently suffice, and the human is still alone. God then, in this version of the creation narrative, creates a woman from the human's rib, not to suggest that she is inferior but rather that the two are alike. The human is pleased and proclaims that "this at last is bone of my bones and flesh of my flesh" (Gen 2:23). It is said "they become one flesh" (Gen 2:24b).

God does later say to the woman that the man "shall rule over you" (Gen 3:16b), but this is by no means a command. That the man shall "rule" here is an observation on the part of God, related to the fact that the two of them, at this point, have disobeyed God's instructions regarding partaking of the fruit of the tree of the knowledge of good and evil. That the man would be punished in that he would have to till the ground for food and that the woman would be ruled by the man are presented simply as facts but not as directions, no doubt reflecting an observation of male-female relationships on the part of the unknown writer. Nevertheless, it is this biblical material that has clearly caused much suffering for women over millennia.[8]

It is in this same description of the creation of woman that we come across what has become a troubling description of woman misread to say she is to be a "helper" to man (Gen 2:18), implying that she is some kind of assistant or subordinate. Here, there is a huge ongoing misunderstanding of the meaning of the term. The current use of the word *helper* in the English language certainly does suggest a subordinate. But the word *ezer* in the Hebrew term עֵזֶר כְּנֶגְדּוֹ (*ezer kenegdo*) (Gen 2:18) does not mean "helper," exactly.[9] So, then, what is the most accurate understanding of this phrase?

Why are we never told that, in the Hebrew Bible, this word *ezer* is employed twice to describe woman, three times to describe powerful

8 Barbara Deutschmann, *Creating Gender in the Garden: The Inconstant Partnership of Eve and Adam*, Library of Hebrew Bible/Old Testament Studies 729 (New York: T&T Clark, 2022), 21–22.

9 Deutschmann, *Creating Gender*, 38.

nations that Israel called upon for help and, very importantly, no less than sixteen times for none other than God?[10] No one perceives God as an assistant, a subordinate, or a help-er! The word means "one who helps," but it connotes a powerful advocate who, like God, comes to protect, resolve problems, and be on your side when you need it the most. Why is this not mentioned in Bible studies and in sermons? How has the suppression of women in relationship to the men in their lives been allowed to continue when the Bible has very clearly named woman as the powerful advocate that man needs to help him get through life? How did we miss this life-giving information all these years? Well, the people who translated the Bible into English somehow decided to give us the impression that, when God is our "help," it means God is a powerful advocate; when the same words describe woman, she is called a help-er, and they imply that she is some kind of lower-level associate. This is simply not the case. The Hebrew word that goes with *ezer*, that is, the word *kenegdo*, is a word that connects the person providing the assistance with the one who receives it, so it can mean something like "*fitting*," or "*appropriate*," or "*comparable*," or "*partner*." Very clearly, the Bible says that women and men were meant to work together, and equally. Any interpretation suggesting the inferiority of women is untenable.

Here are a few traditional translations (emphasis mine):

KJV—"And the Lord God said, it is not good that the man should be alone. I will make *an* [*sic*] *help meet* for him."
MEV—"*a helper suitable* for him."
NLT—"*a helper who is just right for him*."
NKJV—"*a helper comparable* to him."
NRSV—"a *helper as his partner*."

In its verbal form the word *ezer* means "to succor":[11] to offer comfort, solace, consolation, or encouragement. It also connotes strength

---

10 E.g., Exod 18:4; Deut 33:7; 26:29; Ps 20:2; 33:20; 70.5; 89:19; 115:9–11; 121:1–2; 124:8; 146:5; Hos 13:9.

11 BDB 740a.

and power; the one who offers it comes from a position of strength in relation to the other who is, at that time, in need of help.

Let's look now at ways God is described employing this same "helper" word. "The Lord is my help" is found in Psalm 28:7, Psalm 46:1, Psalm 54:4, Psalm 118:7, and Psalm 121:1. So we can see clearly from the context and also from the number of times this word is used to describe God that it does not in any way represent subservience or weakness, or second-class or second-rate behavior. Almighty God is our help or our helper. It means that God is the one who comes to make things right when we are weak! What could it mean for female-male relations if this was understood by those who read the Bible? By naming woman as an *ezer kenegdo* at the outset of the Bible, the female has been set to be for man an advocate, a fitting partner, and someone who is strong enough to come in and get him out of trouble when he needs help. No job description could be more appropriate or uplifting. How, over centuries, have we missed it?

Even when our cultures have placed women in subservient positions and kept them always in a secondary role, women have found ways to rise above their expected situations and manage to command and receive respect.[12]

There are also, strangely enough, instances in the Bible in which man appears to be totally obedient to his woman/wife. A classic example comes early on in Scripture, at Genesis 3:6b, where it says, "She [the woman] took of its [the tree's] fruit and ate; and she also gave some to her husband who was with her, and he ate." At 3:11, God said to the man, "Have you eaten from the tree of which I commanded you not to eat?" At 3:12, the man responded, "The woman whom you gave to be with me, she gave me fruit from the tree, and I ate." There is certainly no sign of male dominance in this passage. The man simply does what he is told!

The man is also totally obedient to the woman in Genesis 21:18–21, in which Sarah demands of her husband Abraham that he cast out

12 André LaCocque, *The Feminine Unconventional: Four Subversive Figures in Israel's Tradition* (Minneapolis: Fortress Press, 1990; repr., Eugene, OR: Wipf and Stock, 2005), 117. Citations refer to the Fortress Press edition.

his slave woman / concubine Hagar and her son Ishmael. In this passage we are told that Abraham did not want to do it, but he does it, nonetheless. We are informed that God tells Abraham it is all right to do so. Either way, however, we hear not a word from Abraham about his own wishes, and we only observe complete compliance on his part to the demand of his wife Sarah. We are told at Genesis 21:14: "So Abraham rose early in the morning, and took bread and a skin of water, and gave it to Hagar, putting it on her shoulder, along with the child, and sent her away. And she departed and wandered about in the wilderness of Beer-sheba." The child and his mother survived their near starvation, not through any action from Abraham, but rather from acts of God on their behalf. One would get no impression whatsoever in this passage that Abraham was wielding any male power. He only acquiesces to the demands of his wife Sarah.

Even though it is true that there is really no place in the Bible where men are specifically directed to control or command women, there is an implicit undercurrent of male dominance. Generally, women do not have autonomy in biblical narratives, but there are several instances in which they use their womanly skills and attributes to get what they need for the good of their families or for the sake of others, their community, and even their people.[13]

One profound example is found in the book of Esther, in which Esther saves all the Jews! When the entire Jewish people is about to be destroyed, it is Esther who comes to its rescue. Young Esther, also known as Hadassah, is encouraged by her kinsman, Mordecai, and under the guidance of the eunuchs of the royal harem where she has been sent, to prepare herself, by means of a variety of beauty treatments over a rather lengthy time, to be chosen to be the queen and new wife of King Ahasuerus of Persia. From this new position of relative power, Esther offers highly appealing banquets for both her husband, the king, and her archenemy, Haman. She gains enough

13 Doreen M. McFarlane, "Wedded to Power: Two Biblical Women Married to Kings," in *Furthering Interfaith Biblical Scholarship: A Festschrift in Memory of André LaCocque*, ed. Doreen M. McFarlane (Eugene, OR: Pickwick, 2024), 130–39.

power to have the evil Haman hanged; her people, the Jews, saved from complete annihilation; and even a position of royal power afforded to her kinsman, Mordecai.

Yet another situation in which a woman may or may not have engaged her womanly good looks and skills to gain power in a biblical narrative is the story of Bathsheba and King David (2 Sam 11:2). Bathsheba, a married woman, is bathing (naked?) and is viewed from the roof by David. David, who has the power to do so, has her brought to him, and the result is that she becomes pregnant. Bathsheba chooses to send David a message saying she is "with child." She is brought to him and, after he has arranged to have her husband sent to the battlefront where he will die, David takes her to be his wife (2 Sam 11:27). The reader is not told of any motives Bathsheba may have had, or, on the other hand, if she has been only the victim of abuse on the part of David. Either way, we learn that, over time, she becomes David's wife and bears the child, and while this child dies, later they become the parents of Solomon (2 Sam 12:24). When David is old and vacillating over whom to make king at his death, we see Bathsheba rising to power. She makes it clear to David that she wants him to choose their son Solomon to become king after him. She does so by reminding him that this is what he had promised her in the past, and he should keep his promise. The biblical text tells us that Solomon "rose to meet her and bowed down to her, and then he sat on his throne and had a throne brought for *the king's mother* and she sat on his right" (1 Kgs 2:19). This text clearly indicates that Bathsheba, at this point at least, has gained and now holds great respect and considerable power.

Both women, Esther and Bathsheba, became wives of powerful kings. Esther, through her newfound power, was able to be responsible for and accomplish the saving of her people, the Jews, from annihilation. Bathsheba was able to get her son Solomon made king when his father, King David, appears to have had other plans. In both cases, the future of the people of Israel was profoundly impacted by these women from powerless beginnings. It was Solomon who built the first temple.

Renowned scholar André LaCocque wrote many books about biblical women and their actions, pointing positively to their lives and behaviors. "It is worth our while," he says, "to reflect on the intrinsic subversiveness of women's interventions in the (biblical) story; a feature so constant in the Bible as to become a principle; one need only think of Sarah, Rachel, Rebecca, Tamar, Deborah, Jael, Ruth, Noadiah (Ez 8:33), Esther, and so many others. . . . Such feminine unconventionality is a powerful counterbalance to the patriarchalism prevalent in some biblical literary genres."[14] LaCocque points out that women such as Esther "confront the enemy face to face . . . [and] tap all the resources of their femininity. . . . The feminine stereotype is left behind, but these women are not transformed into men. They show the way to men without themselves losing their congenital graciousness."[15] Feminist scholar Tikva Frymer-Kensky observes that "there is no 'woman speech' in the Bible; the form of women's argumentation, the nature of their logic and rhetoric are the same as men's."[16] She does note that in order to achieve their goals, powerless women did proceed to work directly or indirectly by means of men with power, convincing and influencing these men to do their bidding. Still, and importantly, she says, "There is nothing distinctly 'female' about the way women are portrayed in the Bible, nothing particularly feminine about either their goals or their strategies." She points out that their goals are the same as those held by the biblical male characters.[17] She notes that "female solidarity and rage are completely absent from the biblical record. Women pursue their goals as actively as men, and use the same techniques and strategies that men in their situation could be expected to use. . . . Most conspicuously, beauty

---

14 André LaCocque, *Esther Regina: A Bakhtinian Reading*, Rethinking Theory (Evanston, IL: Northwestern University Press, 2008), 124.

15 LaCocque, *Feminine Unconventional*, 117.

16 Tikva Frymer-Kensky, *In the Wake of the Goddess: Women, Culture and the Biblical Transformation of Pagan Myth* (New York: Fawcett Columbine, 1992), 146.

17 Frymer-Kensky, *Wake of the Goddess*, 140.

is never portrayed as a woman's weapon. The beauty of women is a mark of divine favor, as is the beauty of men. . . . There are no stories of sexual enticement, no femmes' fatales. . . . There is no woman's toolkit. There are only the strategies . . . used along the various axes of power."[18]

There are many more examples in the biblical texts of women using their gifts and their talents to do good for their families and their community. One example from the New Testament would be that women are said to have supported the ministry of Jesus "out of their own resources" (Lk 8:1–3), and later women were often the first leaders of the church, even offering their homes for the new Christians to gather. Lydia of Thyatira (Acts 16:14–15), likely a successful businesswoman, is remembered as the first recorded convert to Christianity and one who welcomed Paul and his companions into her home. She surely would have been an *ezer* to the early church.

All this said, the women of the Bible did live in a patriarchal society. Contemporary women still understand clearly that it has been a long struggle even to get where we are today. And, still, in our time, it is often those communities that keep to old religious traditions in which women lack autonomy and biblical texts are employed to keep women in line. So it has never been more necessary to shed light on those biblical texts that show God not to be hierarchical and not to want us to behave in hierarchical ways. The texts to show this are present in the Bible but simply have not been used or lifted. They have too often been mistranslated and misread, either intentionally or unintentionally.

According to the Bible, God views women and men as equal partners who are intended to support and help each other as we work together in this world. Our tasks often vary, but one can strengthen the other when each to the other is "bone of my bones and flesh of my flesh" (Gen 2:23).

---

18 Frymer-Kensky, *Wake of the Goddess*, 140–41.

SCENARIO

It could be said that Richard had been raised in a very traditional household. This meant that his father had gone out to work five days a week and labored from nine to five. His dad did not make a lot of money, but somehow it sufficed to pay for the family to live in relatively comfortable circumstances. There were five of them after the three children were born, and Richard was the eldest. As he grew up, he watched his devoted mother do all the cooking, and all the washing and ironing and cleaning. She pickled assorted vegetables and preserved all kinds of fruits, making delicious preserves and jellies. When she had extra time, his mother could be found in the kitchen, baking cookies, cakes, and pies for all to enjoy. The parents would have friends over to play cards on weekends, and Richard's mother would create the finest meals for the family and the guests and enjoyed using all the "good" dishes for those occasions. When not away at work, Richard's father always seemed to find time to help him and his siblings as they grew, teaching them to swim and fish and ride bicycles. Richard was proud of his family. Truth be told, life seemed perfect to him.

When it was time for marriage, Richard, without being intentional about it, looked for someone like his mother; someone he would have described as hardworking and "substantial." Lydia was also pretty and had an excellent sense of humor.

But the world was shifting from under their feet in ways that could hardly be discerned at first. Right from the beginning, Lydia not only wanted to work, but she also *had* to work. It was taking two incomes for them to manage. She didn't mind, but she came to realize that Richard seemed to expect her to meet the standards his mother had been able to keep when housekeeping was her sole duty. They were sensible people but had started arguing about the little things. The two of them decided to see a counselor. After a few sessions and a lot of heartfelt hours of conversation just between the two of them, they came to realize that a lot of their problems had arisen from the ideas they both had held about hierarchy. Without putting words to their thoughts, they had both believed the man should feel solely responsible for the entire family and that, somehow, the woman should be his assistant—his helper—caring for the issues of the home. They'd been taught this over their lifetimes. They'd heard it in church and in society. And their childhood home lives had solidified it in their minds. Although it was never spoken aloud, they had both accepted that woman was somehow second to man. Even at their wedding, it was her father who was expected to "give her away" to the husband. Her father's response when asked "Who gives this woman to be married to this man?" had been "I do." Then Richard had reached to take her hand, and so, it seemed, she had been officially transferred from being the possession of her father to the possession of her husband. And, of course, Lydia had promised in her vows that followed to "obey." Wedding vows had changed considerably in the years that followed, but Richard and Lydia had taken their vows before God seriously.

They wisely decided to go and visit with their pastor to talk more about their situation. Their pastor, who was new to their church, happened to be a woman. She explained to them that, in ancient times, women often stayed home for reasons we would not even think of today. The women kept the fires going and lit the lamps. Women prepared all the food, gave birth, raised children, and kept a home for the men to return to from hunting, warring, and being out in a very dangerous world. She also pointed out that, as Richard and Lydia knew, the tasks of both men and women have dramatically changed in a very different world. Now, in modern times, and especially with many women equally sharing in the responsibility of outside work, it is also certainly time for men to share in household tasks. The pastor showed Richard and Lydia many biblical texts that do present women and men as equal partners. She even explained that the word we have aways translated as "helper" is more often used to describe God and God's relationship with both women and men, and that the word means not "associate" or "underling" but rather a fitting advocate who comes in and gets you out of trouble when needed; an appropriate person to be with you.

Richard loved Lydia and had never intended to lay the responsibility for all the household work on her. It had not occurred to her either, as she had, over time, become overburdened. What had seemed like an appropriate situation for their parents had now changed, as the world and their society was shifting. Lydia was especially pleased that Richard seemed to understand her deep feelings about this issue. And Richard, although feeling pretty guilty, was now more than willing to do his part. They walked out of the pastor's office that day with new hope and started as a genuine team to work on a new plan of action for their marriage. It simply was not 1970 anymore! Both felt the burden of responsibility had been somehow lifted and the joy of sharing every aspect of life together as a new opportunity, even a new adventure. "Equal. Wow." How strange it was that they had never figured that out on their own. It all seemed so obvious.

SO, THEREFORE, WHAT?

We can only dream of what this world could be like (or, better yet, will be like) if we can accept that God intended both women and men from the beginning to be truly equal, and that both women and men could have understood this from the beginning. Each could still have used their individual gifts to lift themselves and each other while also working together in respect and in harmony. The use of individual gifts, if recognized as valued and equal, cannot help but contribute to a better world. Cooperation between the sexes also makes for better lives for all concerned and, of course, for our children.

For centuries in our cultures women have been traditionally put down and kept "in their place." Today, in countless locations throughout the world, women continue to be demeaned, discounted, sexually abused, and in far too many places, even mutilated.[19] But in

---

19 More than 230 million girls and women alive today have undergone female genital mutilation in thirty countries in Africa, the Middle East, and Asia where this is practiced. See Kathrin Weny, Romesh Silva, and Stefanie J. Klug, "Self-Report and Proxy Reports in Survey Data on Female Genital Mutilation,

recent generations, in more and more countries and communities, progress is also being made in creating and building up an environment of equality between the sexes.

We will see in chapter nine, entitled "Embodiment," that in the biblical texts, even God has been sexualized, perceived most often in male terms as a mighty warrior, but (less often) at other times in more feminine language: behaving as a woman might in caring for the vulnerable, giving birth, or assisting in birthing, nurturing, and protecting. Perhaps we will understand God better when we cease separating God and humans by characteristics that are perceived as specifically male or female.

Either way, when women and men are allowed to work together in genuine harmony, the outcome will more likely be peace, success, and satisfaction. These changes can begin to really take effect when we recognize not only that we are equal and can work better together for good, but that God created us to be equal and has always intended us to be that way.

If we had understood the real meaning of the Hebrew word *ezer* (help) from the beginning, our world might be quite different now.

Senegal," Bulletin of the World Health Organization 103, no. 6 (2025): 366–74, https://iris.who.int/handle/10665/381665.

CHAPTER 2

Disagreement

THE QUESTION: WHAT IF GOD DOESN'T EXPECT US TO ACQUIESCE?

Most of us are likely to think that disagreement is a bad thing. We go to a lot of trouble to get along with everyone, and especially with God! But what if God doesn't expect us to always give in? What if God is actually pleased if, in the right circumstances, we are willing to face up to God with our disagreements with God, and argue? Can we let God know when we believe God is not being fair? Are we allowed to misbehave before God? Can we tell God straight out that we believe God is wrong? What are we risking if we are willing to be totally honest in this way before God?

LOOKING AT THE TEXTS

Example One: Job

What may be the carefully hidden but best example of arguing with God can be found in the book of Job. Unfortunately, Job's response to God in the biblical text is often marred by an incorrect, or at least an unexplained, translation. Job has been very angry with God, believing God to be treating him unfairly, and throughout the book of Job, it is very clear that Job remains unwilling to give in. He will not make some kind of insincere confession of guilt. But he also is not at all willing to give up his faith, his trust, and his deep and permanent connection with God. Job fights with God and with his so-called friends relentlessly when he loses his land, his possessions, his health, and (almost all) his family.

When Job and God finally meet for their long-delayed confrontation, what does Job really say to God (Job 42:5–6)? And, even more importantly, what is God's response? There are optional ways to read this text. But you might be surprised! Many of us will have heard over the years about "the patience of Job," but the fact is that, in this biblical narrative, Job displays no patience whatsoever. At the beginning, Job has everything a person of his day could desire, and he is also faithful to God. But, as the story proceeds, Satan makes a wager with God, saying that Job would reject God if all his treasures were taken from him. God says no. God believes Job will remain faithful to him. Then, one by one, everything is taken from Job: his land, his buildings, his animals, his children, and eventually also his own health. Job's response to this is to rail at God for all the harm God is doing to him, and to demand that God come forward and communicate with him directly! Job's so-called friends (Eliphaz from Temen, Bildad from Shuhah, Zophar from Naamath, and the young man Elihu, son of Barakel), appear to represent the typical religious people in this narrative, and they offer him all the well-crafted and expected religious answers. These friends are convinced that Job has done something wrong and needs to apologize to God and make things right, or he is going to be in even bigger trouble. They try everything in their power to talk Job into acquiescing to God, but Job refuses to back off. God has not treated him fairly, he says, and Job demands that God come to him and give him an explanation. The friends, believing that their advice is in Job's best interest, keep trying but without success. They want Job to give in and say he is sorry for whatever sins they believe he has committed. But Job contends that he has not done anything wrong. He refuses to appease God, and he commands God to appear so he and God can discuss this matter face to face. God remains silent for a very long time. Job stands his ground. Finally, God does show up and bullies Job relentlessly, suggesting, "Where were *you* when I laid the foundation of the earth?" (38:4). God goes on and on, reminding Job how very small he is in the scheme of things! For no less than 126 dramatic verses, God makes it very clear to Job that Job had no part in the creation of the world, nor does he have one in the ongoing workings of nature and the universe.

The important issue here is that Job's response to all this at Job 42:6 is very possibly not what our translations tell us. Rather than backing off, giving in, and saying "I relent" or "I despise *myself*" as most of our English translations say, Job may very well be saying to God not "I despise myself" but rather "I despise/pity *you*." Neither the words *myself* nor *you* are in the text at all. Whatever "objective" word fits here, it may be intentionally ambiguous. Does it imply "I despise *myself and repent in dust and ashes*" as so many of our Bible translations give us? Have the translators therefore assumed from the context that Job gave up and told God he, Job, was wrong? Would this mean that Job was sorry for sins he did not commit? Or might it really mean something much more profound? Perhaps Job could have said to God, "I despise *you*!"

From all that God has said here to Job, we certainly could assume that Job is very sorry that he decided to challenge God. After all, God is right in saying to Job that it was God alone who created everything, and that, in relation to the world God has created, Job is as small as a grain of sand on the beach! Still, throughout the text, it is also very clear that God has done Job wrong and, as Job has said, it might be expected and reasonable that an explanation come from God, even though it was not required. Either way, it is also important to remember that throughout the controversy, Job has clung powerfully to the fact that, whatever the outcome, he and God will remain connected. The relationship between God and Job is never in question.

If Job's words were intended to mean "I despise myself" or "I repent," then that may be Job's reasonable response to God's bullying, but it would not really constitute what we could call "good news." Do we have a God who would bully us and then force us into submission? Not good. On the other hand, if Job's words really were intended to mean "I despise you" or "I pity you," then Job is simply giving God a completely honest reply to both the suffering God has heaped upon him, and also to God's relentless bullying. That seems to be not at all unreasonable!

What then, we ask, did Job really say in the narrative, and what was God's real response in this narrative? Importantly, we are informed in the end that God's wrath is not against Job, but against his three friends who had worked so hard to get Job to acquiesce and to do what was considered by them to be the right thing. We may be surprised when God says to the friends, "You have not spoken of me what is right, as my servant Job has" (42:7). Then, to add insult to injury, God tells the friends that Job will pray for them and he will accept Job's prayer. So whatever it was that Job said to God, this was God's response. God is for and not against Job.

It's also important to note that to conclude the story, we are told that God gave Job back twice as much as he had lost (42:10). This may well be some of the best news of the Bible. It would mean that God's love for us extends through our bad behavior, and even through our challenging God. It means we can raise our voices to God when we are sure we are right and even accuse God for God's lack of response. And, if this translation, or even one of the many possible translations, is correct, it means that God will not punish us for our honesty.

Traditional translation: "Therefore I despise [*myself*]."

One other possible/optional translation: "Therefore I despise [*You*, O Yahweh]."

The unvocalized Hebrew verb *'em'as* originally would have had no vowels, so it could be a transitive "I despise" or a reflexive / medio passive "I despise myself" or "I am despised!"[1]

---

1 Naphtali Meshel, "Whose Job is This? Dramatic Irony and Double Entendre in the Book of Job," in *The Book of Job: Aesthetics, Ethics, Hermeneutics*, ed. Leora Batnitzky and Hana Pardes (Berlin: de Gruyter, 2014), 69, doi.org/10.1515/9783110338799.47.

Once one begins digging to find an answer in this case it becomes clear that, as with many other texts in biblical study, Job's answer to God has been a matter of intense scholarly debate over many years, and no final definitive answer has been settled upon by anyone.[2] For those who expect one clear translation for all biblical texts, this can be disconcerting. But, on the other hand, the possibilities in cases like this open to us as readers a real opportunity to grapple with life-affecting issues. We ourselves can begin to ask the questions, and we can ponder on the options open to us. This text is a perfect example. If Job said, "I despise *myself* and I repent in dust and ashes," we may look at this text as showing that, no matter how right we think we are, God is bigger than we are, because only God could have created this world and created us, and we certainly had no part in that creating. And that is okay. But, on the other hand, if we believe that Job may have actually said to God "I despise you" or even "I pity you"—and God still gave Job back everything he had lost (well, most of it[3])—then we can learn the very important lesson for our lives that it really is acceptable to contend with God; that God is big enough to respect and love us when we bare our souls and stand up to him. That is sincere trust. That is real relationship.

The verb *'em'as* does not have a direct object. Therefore, it can also mean something like "I feel loathing," "I hold in contempt," "I repudiate," "I reject,"[4] or "I feel loathing revulsion."

---

2 In *The Book of Job: Aesthetics, Ethics, Hermeneutics*, Naphtali Meshel says, "The ketib-qere in 42 shows the difficulty of deciding who knows what, and the readers of Job 42:1–6 are soon entangled in a web of possibilities that leaves them as ignorant as Job himself. If Job repents at all in 42:6, is he repenting on dust and ashes or of dust and ashes?"

3 Job was, of course, not able to get back the beloved children he had lost. The narrative tells us that he had new children: seven sons and three daughters (Job 42:13). Interestingly, in the text the daughters are said to be beautiful and are named, which is rare in these kinds of stories. They are Jemimah, Keziah, and Keren-happuch. They are said to have received inheritances along with their brothers.

4 John Briggs Curtis, "On Job's Response to Yahweh," *Journal of Biblical Literature* 98, no. 4 (1979): 503, https://doi.org/10.2307/3265665 (hereafter cited in text as *JBL*).

There are three separate cases, the above being one of them, in which the author of Job appears to have "strategically placed extensive double-edged words in the mouths of the characters, allowing [intentionally] for two diametrically opposed readings."[5] This indicates "the artful craftsmanship of the Israelite Wisdom authors" in employing what we might call double-edged irony as "an organizing principle in the Book of Job."[6]

SCENARIO

Lorna and John had just embarked on their first concert tour together. The "concert show" had one soprano (Lorna), one tenor, one baritone (John), and a pianist. It was an operetta-type show and was to be performed for ten weeks: six evenings a week, each night in a different large town or small city. John had hired Lorna, and she had left her entire life behind to sing in this production and to be with John. They had fallen in love. Rehearsing in New York had been hectic, but they'd now been out on the road with three successful performances under their belt. So, other than their ridiculously heavy schedule, everything appeared to be under control.

That fourth morning, they got up early as they had planned to meet John's very old friend Ralph for breakfast. (They were in his city for a performance that evening.) They got in the car and began to drive to the restaurant to meet Ralph when something went terribly wrong. They stopped at a red light and, when the light turned green, John did not drive ahead. Lorna said, "Go. Go!" That was the moment she realized that John's body was not moving. She touched him and his arm seemed stiff. She looked at his eyes and they appeared to be glazed and confused. The light turned red again, then green, then red. Lorna jumped out of the car and rushed over to the driver's side. She pushed John over into the passenger seat, not knowing where her unnatural physical strength had come from. She went back to the

---

5 Meshel, "Whose Job Is This?" 56.

6 Meshel, "Whose Job Is This?" 73.

passenger side and managed to move his legs to that side so she could push him over and climb into the driver's seat herself. A stranger stopped his car and rolled down his window. "How can I help?" he said. Lorna responded, "He's had a stroke. Where is the nearest hospital?" She was in luck, if you could call it that. The hospital was less than a block away. She sped to the Emergency entrance while John lay slumped forward, his head down almost to the floor.

Nurses rushed over, got John into a wheelchair, and rushed him into the Emergency ward. Lorna was hysterical. They told her she'd have to settle down or they'd put her in a hospital bed. "A stroke, a stroke!" she shouted. "He's had a stroke." After about an hour, John had been put to bed, and the doctors came to announce that they believed it was a blocked carotid artery and surgery would be needed. "It may or may not help," they said. Lorna had learned that John, at this point, could not speak, and when he tried, strange, unrecognizable words came from his lips.

There was, it appeared, absolutely nothing she could do. The doctors were planning to operate the next morning to attempt to clean out his carotid. Lorna kept asking herself what on earth she was supposed to do. She called the tenor and pianist to let them know it seemed they would not be going any further until this problem was resolved. And she called the friend, Ralph, with whom they had intended to have breakfast. Then she began to analyze the reality of her situation. As far as things seemed to be going, the tour would be off. Someone would have to pay to fly the tenor and the pianist home to New York. She had left everything in her life behind and for any number of reasons could not return to her old life. She had nothing. If John was not going to get better (and many people who have strokes remain handicapped—even unable to walk or talk), then she would have to be the one to take care of him He could very well be an invalid! She loved him! He had no family to care for him. She was also all he had. Lorna realized that as a singer she had no marketable skills or higher education. So it was simple. She'd be a cleaning woman to provide for them and take care of him when not working. A far cry from the life they had planned together.

It was at this moment that Lorna decided to raise her voice to God. She figured it was a dangerous thing to do but decided she was going to do it anyway. After it was over, she truly did not know if she had been shouting out loud or only in her heart. (She was out on the street at the time.) Strangely enough, at that moment, Lorna didn't even know if she really was a believer or not. But she knew for sure she was going to give God a piece of her mind. "OK, God! Now you listen to me! I've never asked you for a thing. I have tried my best and have never given you any trouble. But this one thing you must do for me. I am furious with you that you would let this happen to me—to us. Yes, I know that human life is like that. Any bad thing can happen anytime. And too often it does! But now? Now, when I finally found my love, after all these years. Now that I have given up everything I had to be with him! Now, when he was perfectly healthy. Right now, when we just started out on our ten-week tour and have all this responsibility! How could you do this to me? I know life is random and anything can happen, but all I have to say to you, big creator of the universe, is this. *Do not do this to me!* Come on. Just make it go away! I cannot do this thing you are asking. Well, all right. Let me say this much. If his stroke is real and he really is disabled, I will do it. I will love him and take care of him, and that will be my life. Ha. Thanks a lot for giving me three whole days of success as a singer. I did enjoy the applause! But the truth is, God, I am not asking you to heal him. I am demanding it. I am shouting at you with all my soul. Do this for me. Do it for him. I do believe that you can do it. And, if I have to be punished for talking to you this way, well then, so be it."

End of rant! Lorna was not even able to stay at the hospital through the surgery the next day. She had to leave with the tenor and the pianist and drive almost a thousand miles to the next venue to do the performance without him. When they stopped for the night, she called the hospital for a report on the results of the surgery. The doctors told her she was in for a surprise. They had been totally shocked when they went in to clear out John's carotid artery; they had found it now to be completely reopened, functioning normally, and not in need of any further work. Totally in amazement about this, they'd simply closed John up again. He was resting back in the room, they told her, and speaking normally again. He would be discharged to rejoin the group in two days.

There never was an explanation. It looked just like a miracle. Many years later, two doctors examined the records and suggested that a migraine may have closed the carotid off for several hours and then, later, it had reopened on its own. Lorna and John's miracle (or non-miracle) gave them another thirty-four years! Either way, Lorna had learned a superb lesson from this nightmare event. And that lesson is that it seems that we can argue with God.

It is a fact that every person's "miracle" is something very personal. People can keep telling each other about the miracle that happened to them, and others will continue being skeptical. The point is that each of us will know in our hearts that the one that happened to us is very real—for us. And that is enough.

Lorna decided in the end that it seems to be true that we can raise our voices to God, even in anger. God is our God after all. And honesty is just part of any real relationship, even the relationship with our Creator. Lorna wondered too, over the many years that followed, how she might have felt about her relationship with God should her beloved have not been healed and if her life had worked out in the negative way she had expected. After all, she understood that things seldom work out the ways that we hope or even expect. She prayed and thanked God quite regularly for the way things had turned out for the two of them because she was always aware that she had done nothing to deserve this reprieve, this second chance. And just because she was so aware that these kinds of miracles are not common, Lorna tried during the years that followed to do whatever she could to help others, to give more generously, and to never forget that too many outcomes are negative, and that, at any given time, many hearts are breaking. She knew too that it would not have been God to blame if things had gone badly. Human life is always precarious, and we need to be grateful for the life that is given to us.

SO, THEREFORE, WHAT?

So, what are we able to learn from this rather complex explanation about God and Job? If, indeed, Job did say something like "I despise you" and God gave him everything back and told Job to pray for his "religious" friends, then this paints a very positive picture of God that we may not have yet considered. *And*, how exciting and life-giving is the idea that we can be free to rail at God about unfair things happening to us and not feel that we need to keep quiet and appease God when God appears to be bullying us. As we see here in the book of Job, if we choose this way of reading it, we note that God is not only forgiving of our very human response, but even willing at times to give us back what we have lost, and even more.

The fact that the biblical text is full of different ways that words and phrases can be translated keeps God's word very much alive and open to us.

Example Two: Elijah's Anger with God

Every person's expression of anger toward God does not conclude with getting one's lost things returned. God is not always going to respond in the same way to each circumstance. So let's look at one very different biblical example.

The prophet Elijah has been very upset with and disappointed in his people. After he has destroyed all the prophets of the god Ba'al, he is still allowed no peace. Queen Jezebel has announced that, within twenty-four hours, she intends to have had him killed (1 Kgs 19:2), so Elijah is required to run for his life. At this point, Elijah, exasperated, proclaims, "It is enough now, O Lord, take away my life" (1 Kgs 19:4b). Is this a shout? We don't know for sure, but we can guess that it is! Presumably exhausted, he falls asleep and is awakened to find that an angel has left food for him. This strengthens him for a forty-day trip to Horeb (1 Kgs 19:8). God asks Elijah what he is doing there and, again, probably in exasperation, he explains to God that his people have forsaken God, and they are out to get him! He is informed that he is to stand out on the mountain because God is about to pass by. He hears a howling wind, but we are told "the Lord was not in the wind." Then there is an earthquake and a fire. The Lord is also not in these. But we are told at 1 Kgs 19:12b, "And after the fire, a sound of sheer silence" (NRSVue), or "the sound of a gentle whisper" (NLT), or the better-known phrase "a still small voice" (NKJV). Only out of the silence or the gentle whisper does Elijah experience the voice of the Lord saying "What are you doing here, Elijah?" Elijah keeps on ranting about how zealous he has been for God and how he has been met only with failure (1 Kgs 19:14). Perhaps to our surprise, God does not strike Elijah down for his failures or for his apparent disappointment in God. God simply and quietly sends Elijah back out into the world with his next set of marching orders. And, we are told, Elijah obeys.

Shouting at God if, indeed, Elijah was shouting has not in this case resolved his very human problems. But neither does it seem to have angered God in any way. There is a profound lesson here, and it is a different but equal lesson about God's response to our honest anger. Here, God has simply, literally and in silence, lifted Elijah up and set him down, back on track.

SCENARIO

Carlos had always been what you might call a "religious man." He had fallen in line after his parents in becoming a respectable, well meaning, gentlemanly person. He had always attended church and by the time he was an adult found himself on the council of his local church and a regular delegate to their synod conventions. He was what one would call upright and responsible. So, then, he felt very much like raising his voice to this God that he'd been so faithful to when practically everything in Carlos's life began to unravel! It all seemed random, but how could so many bad things happen to one person for no apparent reason? Within one year, when Carlos was forty-seven years old, the following occurred. His pastor left to go to a higher-paying church in the city. The new pastor brought in several people who seemed to disagree with every issue that had been going smoothly until then. Carlos's father passed away with cancer. His mother was starting to show the signs of early onset Alzheimer's disease. All this Carlos could handle, it seemed. And then even more personal tragedies started. His teenage son Max was having difficulty at school, and drugs were found in his locker. Carlos's wife, Amara, was furious about this and for no real reason seemed to be blaming Carlos, saying he'd been too hard on the boy. Now she was talking about divorce. (Divorce had never been in his thoughts, ever.) So he did not even know how to begin thinking about such a thing. He felt sure his life was falling apart. He had been a relatively quiet man until then, so raising his voice to God had never seemed an option in any circumstances. But Carlos went out for a walk alone in the country early one afternoon when this was all building in momentum. And out there all alone on a hill, his anger came to a head. He knew he was alone and, to even his own surprise, he just let it all out to God! After all, he had trusted in God all his life. And, yes, like Elijah, Carlos gave God a good talking-to! "Listen, God. I have always been your faithful servant! I go to work. I go to church. I provide for my family. I love them, and I have always loved you. Why? Why are you doing this to me? Yes, yes, I know you never said life was going to be fair! I just expected it from you! Now, God, are you going to fix all this or what?"

As we might expect, the breeze kept blowing, and the sun kept shining, and God remained silent. But, as in the story of Elijah, God did come to Carlos, but in "the still small voice"—in the silence. After all his yelling, Carlos felt a powerful calm come through him, as if he sensed God was saying "Now, Carlos, you can do this thing." And Carlos walked home feeling somehow stronger. God had been with him in good times, and he now felt sure that God was still with him in the bad. As long as God remained with him, things would work out. There was nothing they could not handle together.

SO, THEREFORE, WHAT?

Life issues have a way of working themselves out if we know that God is in all this with us. As everyone knows, God doesn't jump in and solve our problems just because we raised our voice in complaint to him. But God accepts us as we are! Even in the worst situations in which we may find ourselves, we are not alone. The story of God's relationship with Elijah shows us how, even in the worst of times, God was with Elijah and always ready and willing to set him back on track. We learn that no matter how badly things may be going in our lives, God is with us, and there is always a chance for renewal and change.

CHAPTER 3

Repentance

THE QUESTION: WHAT IF GOD IS WILLING TO SAY "I'M SORRY" AND CHANGE DIRECTION?

If God can say "I'm sorry" and change, how would that affect our ability to understand God and, in our own lives, become more willing to say we are sorry and apologize to each other? Too often in the Bible we are reading translations in which God says "I relent" or "I repent" when we would better understand if God simply would say "I made a mistake. I'm sorry." The Hebrew word נִחַם (*nacham*),[1] which means "to be sorry," appears thirty times throughout the Hebrew Bible, and God is said to change God's mind—good news for us.[2] Still, because the English words *relent* and *repent* have been chosen by translators over the words *to be sorry*, we are less likely to really understand. The choice of translation about God's attitude has often shifted away from the more likely meaning, perhaps out of the translator's fear that this would make God look weaker or, in some way, less than perfect.

---

1 BDB 636b.

2 Gen 6:6; Exod 32:14; 1 Sam 15:29; Isa 31:2; Num 23:19; Amos 7:6; Jonah 3:9; Jer 18:8; 26:19; Zech 8:14.

LOOKING AT THE TEXTS

Let us look at and compare four passages in which God is said to relent, repent, turn around, or be sorry.

In Genesis 18:23–33, the narrative tells us that God is greatly disappointed in the people and has decided in response to destroy the great cities of Sodom and Gomorrah. The conversation here between Abraham and God is most interesting. Abraham seems to be the one who has compassion. He tries very hard to get God to change God's mind about the planned destruction, asking "Will you indeed sweep away the righteous with the wicked?" (18:23). Abraham suggests that God really should not do this harm if there are even fifty righteous people in these cities, and God agrees. But Abraham does not give up. He lowers the number to forty-five and makes the request again. God again agrees that it will not be done if there are forty-five righteous ones. Abraham continues to lower the number of righteous to forty, thirty, twenty, and even ten, and God agrees that the calamity will not come upon the cities if there are even ten righteous people there. Unfortunately, according to the story, there must not have been ten righteous people in these cities, because Abraham flees and the cities are destroyed. The message here, nevertheless, is that God has at least been willing to change God's mind and not do the damage if, indeed, even ten righteous people could be found. Most interestingly, in this narrative, it is the human (Abraham) who is being compassionate and God who is listening, reacting, and being willing to change, at least to some extent.

Exodus 32:1–14 tells the story of the people in the wilderness worshipping the golden calf when Moses has gone up to the mountaintop. God, in this story, has every reason to destroy the people that God brought up out of Egypt when, following their rescue, they have forgotten God and, under the leadership of Moses's brother, Aaron, have made for themselves a golden calf that they've begun to worship. While Moses was meeting with God, the people have forgotten that it was God who rescued them from slavery in Egypt. Learning this, God is righteously furious and intends to destroy them. But when

Moses finds out what has happened, he pleads with God on behalf of the people, using a most interesting argument: that God should not do this harm because, if he does, the Egyptians will have won in the end. Moses argues with God that God should not want the Egyptians to think God just brought the people out into the desert to kill them. Moses courageously says to God, "Turn from your fierce wrath, change your mind and do not bring disaster on your people" (32:12). Moses then proceeds to remind God of the promises God has made in the past to Abraham, Isaac, and Israel (32:13). We are then clearly told, "And the Lord *changed his mind* about the disaster that he planned to bring on his people" (32:14). In place of the phrase "changed his mind" (NRSV and NLT), the KJV translates it as "repented," and the ESV says "relented." It is quite clear that the translation that is chosen has some effect on the way the message is received. The English word *relent* means "to become less determined, to give in,"[3] or to change one's mind. But it does not pack the punch of the clear and simple phrase "changed his mind."

In 1 Chronicles 21:15, God is again disappointed in the people and, in this narrative, sends an angel to destroy all of Jerusalem. David and all the elders repent. David reminds God that it is he, David, who is responsible for the sins and he alone who should be punished. He pleads to God, saying "but these sheep, what have they done?" (21:17b). David builds an altar. And God calls off the angel (21:27). David's son Solomon, in response, goes on to build the great temple. Here again, God has repented, relented, or been sorry.

In all of the above narratives, God is angry and disappointed in his people. In all three, the human who holds the power and who is leader of the people (Abraham, Moses, and David) bargains with God and tries to get God to change God's mind. Abraham says the people are innocent and should not be punished along with the guilty, and Moses tries to convince God that the Egyptians will think God had them brought out into the wilderness only to destroy them. David

---

3 *Merriam-Webster Dictionary*, "relent," accessed June 25, 2025, https://merriam-webster.com/dictionary/relent?src=search-dict-box.

says only he is guilty because he takes responsibility for the people's bad behavior. In the first case, Abraham and his family are saved, but the destruction of Sodom and Gomorrah still takes place. But in the Exodus and 1 Chronicles narratives, God changes God's mind, and the destruction does not take place. In the case of 1 Chronicles, David and the elders repent and pay homage to God.

Joel 2:13–14 offers a general statement about the nature and behavior of God, placing some real responsibility for God's choices directly on the behavior of the people. Here is the text.

> "Rend your hearts and not your clothing.
> Return to the Lord your God, for he is gracious and
> merciful,
> slow to anger, abounding in steadfast love, and *relenting*
> from punishment.
> Who knows whether he will not turn and *relent* and leave a
> blessing behind him."

This text suggests that it is always possible for God to change God's mind and turn away from punishing, but it squarely places the responsibility to change and be sorry on the heads of the people.

SCENARIO

Gerry just seemed to be one of those people who could never believe he was forgiven. The result of this was that he had carried the burden of his sins throughout his life. He was in his fifties now, and when he was with others, he often appeared to be somewhat melancholy and not really a happy man. Gerry had what you might call an apologetic demeanor. He often chose not to participate in activities related to the church he attended, and he seldom extended a hand of welcome to newcomers who may have been looking for a friend. He kept to himself, never causing any trouble but also never adding to making any new joys happen.

People who knew him did not want to contribute to his sadness, so they were polite but pretty much left him alone. He came and went from the church and his other activities alone. No one asked Gerry why he was this way. It was just assumed to be his personality. He walked with a cloud over his head, one could aptly say of him.

One day things began to change for Gerry. A woman named Anya, around his age, came to the church, having moved for work from a nearby city. She just walked right up to him at the coffee hour and struck up a conversation. She seemed not to have noticed his somewhat negative "vibes," or at least she had chosen to ignore them. They sat aside from the others, and she gently began to prod him for more information about himself. Instead of pulling away as he often had done in such circumstances, he started slowly to open up. The conversation began with a discussion about the sermon they had just heard. The pastor had pointed out that we are infinitely loved by God and that, in the Bible, God changes God's mind more than once and stops whatever calamity God had planned. Anya suggested that this means all of us are worthy of being rescued. "A lot of people think God is angry with them," Anya pointed out. "I thought for years that God was angry with me; that is, until I came to realize that I was feeling that way because I had not been able to forgive myself for something." Gerry found himself really being attracted to this woman, even before she spoke these words. But at that moment, it was as if a floodgate had opened. Unspoken thoughts came pouring in on him. "Unable to forgive oneself?" That could have been what was holding him back all these many years. Gerry's father had been unforgiving of almost every childish mistake Gerry had made. The words *I'm sorry*, when they had come from Gerry's lips, had never been met with words of forgiveness. Gerry, over the years, had carried guilt, although unspoken, for every little mistake he had made. He did not want to blame his father, who himself had had a difficult life. Gerry's mother had been quiet and acquiescent to his dad. He had no siblings to tell him what he had done was not so serious. Gerry had just become quiet. As a young adult he had tried drugs once. Nobody really knew this, but he felt that old guilt and it slipped deep beneath the surface. He'd gone to college for a year and then dropped out. He blamed himself for this as well, thinking he'd not tried hard enough when the real reason was that he, like many of his peers, had chosen a course of study that was just not right for him. Guilt, it seemed, had secretly simply become a way of life for Gerry.

As it turned out, it was the combination of that Sunday's sermon on God being sorry and changing God's mind combined with that first enlightening conversation Gerry had at the coffee hour with his new friend Anya that was the beginning of his turning around. You see, there was nothing wrong with Gerry other than that Gerry did not feel very good inside about himself. This feeling had manifested itself into his becoming a sad and, consequently, a lonely man. Anya did not become his wife or even his girlfriend. But she became his good friend. Whenever they were in church, at a Bible study class, or a social event, she would be quick to remind him that it's OK to be sorry, but it's also OK to forgive yourself and to change and move on. She always made light of it, almost as if it were a joke. But she could see in time her melancholy friend turning into a more joyful person. Gerry had learned in church that one Sunday how very much God loves humankind and how sorry God is if we are ever hurt or hurting. From that time, Gerry found a thousand reasons to be happier with his life. Maybe, all those years back, his father had not known how to be sorry and forgive him, but now Gerry knew how to forgive himself. Perhaps even more importantly, Gerry had found a place in his heart to forgive his father. Sunshine was coming into his life.

SO, THEREFORE, WHAT?

We can clearly see from looking at the above biblical passages that God, although unchanging in God's nature, is in certain circumstances indeed willing to change God's mind, willing to be sorry, and willing to go in a new and different direction. Sometimes it is because a biblical character has talked God into forgiveness on behalf of the people. And often God changes God's mind because the people have been visibly sorry for their behavior. The question for us is this. How might our reactions related to being sorry, repenting, and forgiving others and ourselves be different if we come to understand that the texts do translate into English that God truly was sorry and that God is willing to change God's mind?

Translators may have been somewhat unwilling to say that God can be sorry because they have been trying to deal with other passages in which it is written that God is totally stable and therefore does not ever change. Isaiah 40:8 says of God, for example, "The word of our God will stand forever." Malachi 3:6 says, "For I the Lord do not change." And, in the New Testament, Hebrews 7:24 says of Jesus that "he holds his priesthood permanently because he continues forever." Hebrews 13:8 says, "Jesus Christ is the same yesterday and today and forever." How can we interpret the fact that we have been clearly taught in such texts of scripture that God is unchangeable, and this has even constituted a strong trust in which we live? Probably this is the reason why the English word *relent* tends to be used by translators to avoid suggesting that God's earlier decisions were ever in error. But this really has little or nothing to do with unchangeability in God's nature. It should be very good news for us to learn that God, indeed, is able to turn around on any plans God may have made to punish the people, and that God's unchanging compassion and undying love for us allows God to, when appropriate, even be "sorry" for having considered punishing us! This good news means that God truly does love us and wants the best for us.

We know, in our own human relationships, that being sorry and being willing to change our minds and to forgive is not always easy. But it is a powerful part of moving toward being more loving and, ultimately, often being more deeply loved by those who have been forgiven. Being sorry and being forgiving and forgiven are profoundly important aspects of love. In the Bible, God models this. This suggests that it may be the same for God, in that willingness to change God's mind and to forgive enables consistency of character. We are created, after all, in the image and likeness of God.

The point is that God can be unchanging in nature while still being willing to say "I'm sorry" and turn in another direction. This is something many of us have not considered in the past. Too often we forget that God's nature is to be loving always. Often, as we have seen in this chapter, it is because of God's unchanging, loving nature that God is indeed willing to be sorry and to not do any harm to God's beloved people. This reminds us of a kind of chant that many Christians like to repeat in private and in public church-related gatherings. It is simple but it is life-giving. "God is good . . . all the time. All the time . . . God is good!"

Too often in the past, because our biblical translators have been reluctant to make it clear that God really was sorry, we have missed out on being willing to be sorry ourselves for the ways in which we have hurt others.

CHAPTER 4

Enemies

THE QUESTION: WHAT IF OUR ENEMIES ARE NOT GOD'S ENEMIES?

In the Hebrew Bible / Old Testament, our enemies are those who do not like us or those who want to do us harm, but never those whom we do not like or for whom we want to do harm. The word we have translated as "enemy" means "one who hates." The Hebrew word is אוֹיֵב (*oyebh*)—"one who shows hostility to"[1]—and occasionally צַר (*tsar*), which means approximately the same—"someone who distresses me."[2]

But how would we treat those we perceive as our enemies if we knew they were doing the best they could? This is a profound question because, even though we are always told that God loves us and God loves all people, we secretly still tend to assume that those we are against are also people that God must be against. As an example, during World War II, the Americans and the British certainly, and for good reason, would have seen God as on their side of the conflict. Yet at the same time, we have learned that the Nazi SS soldiers were provided with belt buckles that had written on them the German words *Gott mit uns* (God with us)! The origin of this phrase goes back

1 BDB 33a.

2 BDB 849a.

to a medieval Teutonic Order and was also inscribed on military helmets and belt buckles during the First World War.[3] Needless to say, wars and World Wars exude the epitome of evil, none of which surely the Deity would condone. But this is just to point out that most every group perceives itself as having God on its side. The average German soldier, at least at the beginning, quite likely perceived himself as a good and patriotic person, even protecting his country from enemies. Misperception of who one's "enemies" are can lead to devastation.

At Jeremiah 32:27, God claims to be God of all humankind. "See, I am the Lord, the God of all flesh; is anything too hard for me?" Yes, it is true that evil exists in this world. There are few of us, and certainly few, if any, nations that can say they do not have enemies. Still, it is dislike and hatred that perpetuate war and subsequently much suffering in our world. Indeed, we are responsible to try to the best of our ability to bring about harmony in both our individual lives and in our world. It is our call by God to make friends of those we perceive as enemies if possible.

LOOKING AT THE TEXTS

The Others/Enemies in the Story of Jonah

Jonah is a prophet of the Lord in the biblical book titled with his name. It seems clear at the outset that God's goal is to send Jonah to call the people of Nineveh to repent and turn to God. But Jonah, apparently, does not care for these Ninevites, and the last thing Jonah seems to want is for them to repent and be approved of by God! God says to Jonah: "Go at once to Nineveh, that great city, and cry out against it, for their wickedness has come up before me" (Jonah 1:2). Nineveh was an ancient Assyrian city. The prophets Zephaniah (2:13–3:9) and Nahum had prophesied the destruction of Nineveh.

3 "Gott mit uns und wir mit ihm!" *Collections Spotlight* (blog), The National WWI Museum and Memorial, accessed June 25, 2025, https://www.theworld-war.org/learn/about-wwi/gott-mit-uns-und-wir-mit-ihm.

Nahum speaks of Nineveh's sins as the following: plotting against God (1:9, 11), idolatry (1:14), vile behavior (1:14), shedding blood, lying, and plundering (3:1), enslaving nations (3:4), presumption (3:8), and cruelty (3:19). According to the book of Jonah, the city had about 120,000 citizens, and it would take three days to walk through it. So it would seem clear (if the Jonah story and that of Nahum would agree) that God would have every reason to hate, and maybe even want to destroy, the Ninevites. Jonah appears to despise the Ninevites. God, on the other hand, desires that the Ninevites repent and turn to God. The message seems clear, in the narrative of Jonah, and in various texts throughout the Bible, that our enemies are not necessarily God's enemies. "The Lord is gracious and merciful, slow to anger and abounding in steadfast love. The Lord is good to all, and his compassion is over all that he has made" (Ps 145:8–9).

Jonah chooses to board a ship going in the opposite direction from Nineveh, the place where God is calling him to go. Let's look now at the pagan sailors on the ship Jonah has boarded, trying to go to Joppa, and observe what the sailors' faith leads them to do. They are not classic "enemies" in this story, but they do not share faith in the God that Jonah worships. Early on, when the storm is beginning, we are told that the mariners were afraid and "each cried to *his god*." Instead of throwing Jonah overboard, they throw out their own cargo to lighten the load (Jonah 1:5). Jonah does nothing whatsoever to help, but instead chooses to make his way down to the hold of the ship, where he lays down and falls asleep. The mariners find him there, and the captain demands that he "Arise, call upon your god!" (1:6). The mariners cast lots and determine that Jonah is indeed responsible for the storm. They accuse Jonah and ask him what they can do to him so the sea will calm down. Note that, instead of making demands on Jonah, they are asking him what they should do. Strangely, Jonah responds that they should pick him up and throw him into the sea (1:12). Do they follow his suggestion immediately for their own survival? No! We are told the mariners instead rowed hard to bring the ship back to land (2:13). This is not the response from them that the reader would expect. After all, these are not followers of Yahweh. Their very lives are at stake in this storm, and they have no reason whatsoever to protect Jonah. The next thing the sailors do is again remarkable and unexpected. We are told that they pray to Jonah's God that they should not have to throw him overboard, and then, later, the sailors sacrifice to Jonah's God, all while Jonah does nothing to save himself or them. "Then they cried out to the Lord 'Please O Lord we pray, do not let us perish on account of this man's life. Do not make us guilty of innocent blood, for you, O Lord, have done as it pleased you'" (1:14).

It is very clear that these pagan sailors do not want the life of Jonah on their heads. Finally, against their own will and in total desperation, they do toss Jonah into the sea, and the mighty storm is assuaged. They must have also decided, at this point, that they now have considerable respect for Jonah's God. We are told they then feared the Lord (Jonah's God) and "even more, they offered a sacrifice to the Lord [Jonah's God] and made vows" (1:16). So, it seems, we have an entire shipload of converts to Yahweh, Jonah's God, without his having lifted a finger. Is this the way we'd expect "enemies" to behave? No!

The average churchgoer, even Sunday school children, would very likely be able to relate to certain portions of this incredible tale of Jonah. From what most of us have been taught, the point of the entire story, for us, would likely be that Jonah was running away from God and that he spent three days in the belly of a whale or fish.[4] The story would be about a prophet who found that he could not run away from his calling. This is all well and good, but few seem to notice (and this may also be a good part of the delightful comedy of the narrative) that while Jonah, God's prophet, is actively running away from his calling, the sailors, worshippers of other gods, continue to do everything in their power to protect Jonah and to keep from having to throw him into the sea. They are practical in not wanting his death on their heads, but, in this story, these sailors are doing everything

4 The word refers to a big fish, although traditionally we have been told it was a whale.

right while Jonah is doing everything wrong. These sailors are not exactly enemies, but they, like the Ninevites, are people for whom Jonah has little or no concern. The writer of this story, instead of speaking ill of them or putting them down, seems to make a special effort to show us how so-called pagans, nonbelievers, worshippers of "other" gods, or "enemies," may still be doing all the right things.

In the end, the sailors are compelled to throw Jonah into the sea, but they only do so reluctantly. God finds a way to protect Jonah, albeit a strange one. This narrative presents us with an opportunity to consider the actual behavior of people whom we may perceive as enemies, or, at the very least, strangers.

Jonah, after spending time inside the "big fish," is vomited out onto the land. (Yes, speaking of translation, the word is not *thrown* but really is *vomited*!) As the narrative progresses, the reader can sense that Jonah still does not want the Ninevites to repent. We are told the city takes three days to walk through, but Jonah doesn't seem to want to go out of his way and only walks one day's distance. He does not exactly ask them to repent, but only threatens them, saying at 3:4b, "forty days more, and Nineveh shall be overthrown." Probably to his surprise, Jonah finds that they sincerely repent. And God does save them. The most interesting message for us here is that "God changed his mind about the calamity he had said he would bring upon them, and he did not do it" (3:10b).

God appears to care about the pagan sailors, and, also, the enemy Ninevites. As we've seen in the previous chapter, God is willing to change God's mind. God also seems to forgive his own reluctant prophet Jonah because, when Jonah is pouting, God grows a plant up over him to shield him from the sun (4:6). Jonah is still not happy. The story ends with God pointing out to Jonah that Jonah does not have his priorities straight. Still, Jonah seems to see himself as being in competition with his perceived enemies.

The narrative of Jonah gives us opportunities to observe two sets of "others"—the sailors and then the Ninevites—in both cases clearly behaving better than God's own prophet Jonah. And, importantly, God is calling us to care for them too. The very last sentence of the book has God challenging Jonah, who has been selfish and insensitive throughout the narrative. God says the following to Jonah: "And should I not be concerned about Nineveh, that great city, in which there are more than a hundred and twenty thousand persons who do not know their right hand from their left and also many animals?" (4:11). This profound closing sentence for the book of Jonah seems too often to have been ignored by readers. It cries out to us that God does care for our enemies! God wants them to repent. And God wants Jonah and all of us to care for them too (and even their animals), so that, in time, they will turn to God.

"Other Biblical Enemies"

Some enemies of Israel in the Hebrew Bible were the Philistines, Edomites, and Moabites, mainly due to what is described as their worship of idols. The people of Israel were directed not to follow in their behaviors but to remain faithful to their God.

The Moabites were enemies of Israel (Judg 3:28), yet God used them to accomplish divine plans. The point of these stories is to show that God works in mysterious ways to make entire nations do God's will. Another classic individual example is King Cyrus of Persia, who was no believer in the God of Israel. Yet it was after his conquering of Babylon, that the people of Israel were, in time, allowed to return home after the exile. It was Cyrus who sent them back and even allowed them to take with them the sacred vessels and money for rebuilding the temple.[5] For this reason, the Bible states "Thus says the Lord to his anointed, to Cyrus, whose right hand I have grasped to subdue nations before him and to strip kings of their robes . . . so that you may know that it is I, the Lord, the God of Israel who call you by your name" (Isa 45:1–3). You may note here that God even calls Cyrus, the enemy king, his "anointed," which is the same word in Hebrew as *messiah*. This is in the context of being chosen to accomplish a task. Throughout the Hebrew scripture Israel deals with

5 This, however, is questioned today by scholars.

nations and groups who live and worship differently from themselves. Some are enemies. It is usually said that God battles either on the side of the Israelites or, in some instances, even on their behalf. For example, at Exodus 23:22b–23a, it is said by God, "I will be an enemy to your enemies and a foe to your foes. When my angel goes in front of you and brings you to the Amorites, the Hittites, the Perizzites and the Canaanites, the Hivites and the Jebusites, and I blot them out, you shall not bow down." Deuteronomy 20:3b–4 says, "Do not lose heart or be afraid or panic or be in dread of them, for it is the Lord your God who goes with you, to fight for you against your enemies to give you victory."

Although the biblical narrative says the Canaanites were annihilated, genetic research indicates that any such slaughter was likely to have been part of the biblical story rather than any kind of historical account.[6] The Israelites, historically, appear to have simply been one group who lived in Canaan, among many others. What about the Amorites? Historically, these people lived in Mesopotamia and ended by 600 BCE. And Hittites? They ended in the outgoing second millennium BCE. The biblical account of the writing of the Exodus narrative is not possible to date because it has not been possible to match it up with the historical accounts of related matters that we do have.[7]

SCENARIO

Jonathan grew up in a small town and did not even realize he had been raised in an environment of prejudice. He'd often heard his parents and grandparents speaking negatively about the people who had immigrated to their neighborhood in the past ten years. This talk was generally subtle, and no one would have been likely to have

6 Christian Frevel, *History of Ancient Israel* (Atlanta: SBL Press, 2023), 81, https://doi.org/10.2307/JJ4470334.3.

7 Frevel, *History of Ancient Israel*, 76.

openly accused them about the way they talked. These immigrant people were described by his family and friends at times as lazy, as contentious, as unattractive, and more. Jonathan had never given the issue much thought and had decided to stay out of it. After all, this negative talk did not seem to affect him in any way.

Over the years, Jonathan found himself in multiple interactions with these newer neighbors. They were mostly his fellow students in school. And, yes, some of them had trouble keeping up because they had come from another country and had to struggle with a new language. There were also many cultural differences. As they moved into their teens, Jonathan just fit in, while these young immigrants never seemed to have the right clothes, the right moves, or the right chatter. Jonathan came to realize, over time, that some of his best friends seemed to hold the same negative ideas about them as his parents had expressed at home. Again, he chose to say nothing.

There was, however, one young woman in his class who came from the other culture—the immigrants! Jonathan began to feel, over time, that he might want to care for her in some special way. And the young woman, Sulla, appeared to be feeling much the same. As he began spending time with her, he came to learn so much. Over a few months, he found out that the behaviors that his parents and friends had judged negatively about these people came from very realistic and practical reasons. For one, they'd been criticized for keeping to themselves, especially the older folks. The reason was they were finding it difficult to learn the new language. They often kept to themselves because they were shy about making mistakes in conversation. The young people were often criticized because they did not attend all the parties and special events offered by the school. Their reasons were often that they were nearly always working part time with extra jobs for their families just to make ends meet. Their eating habits were different because that was the food they'd eaten in their previous country. As Jonathan came to know Sulla, he began to learn and appreciate more and more about her homeland and culture. These same people who his family and friends had viewed as "other" were those who Jonathan, in time, came to see as genuine friends. At the same time, Sulla began to view Jonathan's culture as less frightening.

These kinds of situations, in relation to culture clashes, generally change greatly over one or two generations. People who see each other as enemies are often people who do not understand each other. There are situations in which one person, or even one nation, is trying to overcome the other. There is often both need and greed involved in such cases.

Jonathan was invited to dinner at Sulla's home. That night, Sulla's father, who loved to complain and moan about the war zone from which he had been able to rescue his family, was particularly talkative. Jonathan had a little trouble understanding Sulla's father, but he was able to pick up enough information through her dad's broken English to realize that Sulla's family, and many of the other immigrants Jonathan had known from school, had literally run for their lives. They had been fortunate enough to be welcomed into a safe country. They were still traumatized but always beyond grateful for the opportunities the new country afforded them. Most importantly of all, Jonathan could see for the first time that these people were still under great pressure and definitely doing their best—their very best—to make a good life for themselves and to fit in. He realized too that they were still quite exhausted from the pain they had suffered back home and from the big learning curve they'd been on. But, most importantly, Jonathan realized that they were good people. The immigrants were not the enemy in any way.

Jonathan was still a young man. He was not sure how he was going to try to help his family and his other friends to understand. Seeing these people as "other" and as enemies had been a real mistake. There was room in Jonathan's big country for them all. People whose families had been here longer were no better than those who had arrived recently. It was just harder, much harder, to be a new member of a country and of a community than for those whose families had been here for generations.

It is not always the case, of course, that strangers or enemies become friends, but it can and does happen. A few weeks later,

Jonathan heard from his pastor in a sermon about Jonah and the Ninevites. He listened to the story of Jonah with a new perspective and couldn't help laughing to himself, thinking "Oh, that Jonah! He probably just didn't understand those Ninevites. It's a good thing God, as usual, knew what he was doing." At that time, Jonathan became even more determined that he would help his family and friends to understand. And, in time, he did.

SO, THEREFORE, WHAT?

The issue of God's behavior with strangers and enemies in the biblical text gives us the opportunity to consider whether we really know the God of the Bible as well as we may have thought we did. The point is that, although at times in the biblical texts God has promised to fight alongside us or even on our behalf, our enemies are not necessarily always God's enemies. And, more importantly of course, we know that God is the God of all people—God of those who know God and of those who do not. Jonah admits he is already very much aware of this when he says, "For I knew that you are a gracious and merciful God, slow to anger, abounding in steadfast love, and relenting from punishment" (4:2).

How will we go forward if we come to realize more clearly that our enemies or adversaries are not hated or disliked by God? For one, might we be able to learn from God as a role model of patience and forgiveness? Could we ever change our enemies into friends or even, over time, unite our religious communities with others that are different and create ecumenical communities? Yes, of course, there is evil in the world, and we cannot give in to this kind of behavior. Without question, Satan is, indeed, always the enemy of good. But misunderstanding as evil or even as "other" those many individuals and communities who are simply different from us can only prevent us from allowing space for love—God's kind of love—to emerge and to grow.

CHAPTER 5

Love

THE QUESTION: WHAT IS THE REAL MEANING OF GOD'S LOVE?

How can understanding God's kind of love affect our relationships with each other? What if we could learn to love as God loves: freely and magnanimously?

Far too often, churchgoers will casually remark that the so-called Old Testament God is full of wrath and suggest then that it was only with Christ that love came into the world. To be sure, there are negative and violent stories in Hebrew scripture. But the fact is that Hebrew scripture speaks regularly and clearly from the beginning about the love and protection from God, who really cares for all people.

To begin, in our culture and our times, the word *love* has been twisted in every direction. We love to talk about love. We celebrate Valentine's Day and send each other cards, chocolates, flowers, and other gifts to show our love. Most often this is romantic love, and the term expresses a warm feeling or sentimental emotion. All well and good. But, in the Bible, the word *love* very often relates not only to emotions but rather to matters of social justice and of helping those who need assistance. This is especially true in the prophetic books and in particular the books of Micah and Hosea.

In parts of the biblical text, God expresses love profoundly toward the people of Israel, describing God's self as being a husband to Israel. Words about this kind of love are employed at Hosea 2:16–20a: "On that day, says the Lord, you will call me 'my husband' . . . I will make you lie down in safety. And I will take you for my wife forever . . . in righteousness and justice; in steadfast love and in mercy. I will take you for my wife in faithfulness, and you shall know the Lord." This passage is a magnificent example of God's love, expressed using the metaphor of marriage. As the book of Hosea the prophet continues, the people of Israel are described as cheating on God by worshipping other gods. At Hosea 11:1–4, the relationship is described alternatively with God as a parent, saying "When Israel was a child, I loved him, and out of Egypt I called my son. . . . Yet it was I who taught Ephraim to walk; I took them up in my arms, but they did not know that I healed them. I led them with cords of human kindness, with bands of love. I was to them like those who lift infants to their cheeks. I bent down to them and fed them."

LOOKING AT THE TEXT

In many languages, it takes more than one word to describe a concept. Just as an example, in the languages of the Inuit people of North America, there are believed to be fifty or more different words related to snow, some representing, for example, "snow on the ground," "falling snow," "drifting snow," "soft deep snow," "snowbank," and more! In Biblical Greek, there is the word *eros* representing human emotional love, *agape* for the highest form of charity, and *philia* for brotherly (sisterly) love.

In other cases, one word takes many words to say in another language. In the Danish language, there is the word *huyge.* Danish people understand much when this one little word is spoken. It encompasses such things as a cozy and content feeling people get when enjoying life's simple pleasures, being with others that one cares about, and joyfully sharing food and drink. The word can be traced back to an old Norse word in the Middle Ages that meant "protected from the outside world."

A second example is the Icelandic word *auminge*. It can mean something negative like a loser or a weakling. Yet this word is used more fondly when speaking about poor or elderly people and often when speaking about a child, indicating vulnerability or helplessness, but it is spoken in a sense of gentle kindness and caring. It would be difficult to express the meaning of this word except in context and also by the tone of voice when speaking it, because the meaning can vary so widely.

There are several different words for love in Biblical Hebrew. The Hebrew word אהב (*'aheb*)[1] appears over 200 times and is intense and sometimes sexual. Also, חֶסֶד (*hesed*) or loving-kindness,[2] another word for love or steadfast love, appears 250 times and represents a love given freely, magnanimously, without expectation of return. We are admonished to love each other in this manner. We will take a closer look at these two Hebrew words for love.

There are other words for love that appear much less frequently in the Bible. These include the following:

דוד (*dod*) means "beloved"; it can represent the man in a relationship in which marriage is contemplated. It appears about twenty times in the Hebrew Bible but occasionally means "uncle."[3]

רַעְיָה (*ra ya*) means "female companion," "friend," or "neighbor," and it is found only in Song of Songs.

יָדִיד (*yadid*) is employed to denote someone who is cherished, conveying deep affection and endearment. It is also used in the context of close relationships, such as between friends or within a family. In the biblical context, it can also refer to the beloved status of Israel or individuals in

1 BDB 12b–13a.
2 BDB 338b.
3 BDB 187b.

their relationship with God. It appears as an adjective nine times in the Hebrew Bible and as "my/your/his beloved" five times. It can also mean "lovely" as in Psalm 84 and as a feminine plural in Psalm 45.

חָשַׁק (*chashaq*) is a rare verb; it can represent a desire of one person to permanently be attached to another; meaning something like "bind together," which describes God's love for Israel in Deuteronomy 7:7 and 10:15. The word appears eleven times in the Hebrew Bible.

רֶחֶם (*rechem*) means "compassion" or "mercy," and it is also the word for a woman's womb. This word appears twenty-six times in the Hebrew Bible and is also used to indicate compassion.

Moving back to the word אהב (*'aheb*), meaning "love," we've noted that this word appears in the Hebrew scripture two hundred times. It can but does not always mean intense attraction for the opposite sex. An example is Amnon's "love" for Tamar (2 Sam 13) which, in that context, sounds more like "lust." This word more often describes a positive relationship such as the love that leads to marriage, like Jacob's love for Rachel (Gen 29:18), a family bond such as Ruth for Naomi (Ruth 4:15), or that of a parent for a child such as Rebekah for Jacob (Gen 25:28). This word is also used to describe a relationship that includes political loyalty. David is loved by Saul (1 Sam 16:21) and by Jonathan (18:1). It is said that Jonathan loved David as he loved himself. This represents more than a political bond. It represents a commitment of some kind. Some people are said to love things they shouldn't such as wine (Prov 21:17) or silver (Eccl 5:10). This word, '*ahev*, can also be used for love of abstract qualities: righteousness (Ps 45:8), God's commandments (Ps 119:47), or wisdom (Prov 29:3). You will remember that this word for love is also found (in Greek of course) in the mouth of Jesus in the synoptic gospels at Matthew 19:19, Mark 12:31, and Luke 10:27, the love word being the Greek word *agape*. In Hebrew scripture, the one who loves is often also the גֹּאֵל (*goel*) or "redeemer": the person who gets you out of trouble when you can't get yourself out. So the word is often directly related to practical action on the part of the person who loves, toward the person whose needs are being met because of this love. This word, *'aheb*, is used for God's relationship with Israel and Israel's love for God. The famous Shema in Deuteronomy 6:4–5 says: "You shall love the Lord your God with all your heart, and with all your soul [whole being (*nephesh*)] and with all your might." In Deuteronomy, love is spoken of in relation to the Sinai covenant and means not just intimate affection but obedience to God's commandments and loyalty to God alone. The roots of this covenant-related meaning of love probably come out of Near Eastern secular political terminology. God's people are called to love the neighbor (Lev 19:18) but also the stranger (Lev 19:34; Deut 10:19). Israel's history strongly emphasized giving help to those in need, especially the people who are weak and underprivileged. The Bible says that God loves Israel, and this love includes God's choosing and rescuing the people of Israel. God continues to love Israel even though it makes mistakes (Jer 31:3). "I have loved you with an everlasting love."

The other most-used word for love in Hebrew scripture is חֶסֶד, (*hesed*), a noun with no verbal counterpart that appears 250 times in Hebrew scripture. This word is not always translated into English as "love." Rather, it represents love in action: loyalty, steadfastness, loving-kindness, devotion, faithfulness, mercy, goodness, and being in covenant relationship. This word requires action and commitment and is always something we do—real acts that rescue or uplift people who need help. Scholars used to think that the word was only connected with laws and was only a kind of legal word. It is now understood not as being about equals giving to each other but, instead, to be about relationship. For *hesed* to be happening, one party must be in need and the other must choose to supply that need. You cannot have *hesed* (love) for wine or silver or money because they cannot return your love. This kind of love involves helping those who are circumstantially weaker. It refers to the relationship in which the stronger person strengthens or rescues the weaker. The goal is also to build up society. The word *hesed* means active concern for the well-being of all people by building up those who are poor or who have no voice in society. It represents rescue and protection of the marginalized. In Hebrew scripture, these poor people are often named as the widow and the orphan, the alien or the stranger in the land.

The word *hesed* also implies the need for good courts and systems of justice. In *hesed*, the person in need cannot perform the action, and help is essential (the person in need will often suffer badly if help is not forthcoming). One person has no other way of getting help and the other is able to provide the needed assistance. The one in need has no control over the decision of the person who can help, and there are no legal sanctions for not helping. If the person does not choose to provide *hesed*, this kind of act of love, probably no one will even know. In other words, for the act to constitute *hesed* love, the helper must make a free moral decision to do so, without the chance of being rewarded or honored for it. (This reminds us of Jesus when he said we should give our help and say our prayers in secret in Matthew 6:6–7.) So, as you can see, the English words *love*, *loyalty*, *kindness*, and *mercy* are all part of the meaning of *hesed* love, but they do not contain the whole meaning.

Examples of the word *hesed* in Hebrew scripture are in Psalm 23:6, often translated here as "mercy," the "steadfast love" of Psalm 69:13 and 1 Chronicles 16:34, and as "kindness" in Proverbs 31:26 (NRSV).

A relationship does not have to be personal for *hesed* to be given or requested. Often the person asking for it has previously been able to give it but now is not. The central features for *hesed* are the situation of critical need on the part of one person, the unique opportunity to assist on the part of the other, and the freedom of decision.

SCENARIO

Raymond knew one thing right from the beginning. He knew deep down in his heart that the church's offer of breakfast every day had no strings attached. He knew this partly because just about everything else he supposedly got for free was, in the end, far from free!

For one, there was another church in town that would feed him if he listened to their preaching and promised to read the Bible verses that they handed him. He didn't mind listening and reading. But there was something about the "no strings" policy that left him at least with a shred of dignity.

Raymond didn't make excuses for how he'd ended up homeless and without funds. He understood he had a good deal to do with all his failures in life. He had tried hard to hold on to at least some of his dignity. There were many days when he simply did not have the energy or the will to look for a job. But, still, he believed he was trying!

Raymond was seldom surprised, but one day at the breakfast, he did have a real surprise. He went up to the counter and picked up a bowl of cereal, some toast, and coffee. He located an empty table and sat down alone, expecting or at least hoping to stay alone. The fellow patrons were generally not his favorite people. But that day, an older man came and sat at the other end of the table, leaving Raymond the space he'd hoped for. The man introduced himself as Jeff and mentioned how much he appreciated these free breakfasts. Raymond perceived Jeff as a kind of "religious" guy. He talked a fair amount about God but not in any kind of preachy way. He was just expressing to Raymond the things he was happy about. Wasn't it a glorious sunny morning? Didn't this cereal always taste so good? And the coffee wasn't bad either! Raymond listened, quietly at first, but then began to talk about some of the few good things in his life. Jeff had certainly put Raymond into a better frame of mind, right from the get-go.

To add to the good things happening that day, Jeff put Raymond onto a possible day-job location. He gave Raymond the name of a church he'd not heard about that served a decent dinner once a week. He told Raymond where he was staying and said quite seriously, "I don't have much, but please know I will help you if I ever can. I'm just barely on my feet right now, but I know I will be." He finished off his breakfast and disappeared out the door. Raymond sat there, astounded. This stranger had talked about God's unending love and how God gives that love freely without expectation of return. Raymond wondered if this Jeff had even realized that the concern for him that he was showing was a direct sign of that love God had given him. Raymond knew he himself had believed he had absolutely nothing to give to others. Now it occurred to him that maybe everyone has something to give. He hadn't figured out just what it was he had to give, but if a stranger could care at all, then maybe he too could care for others. He knew there were many people in even worse conditions than he was. Maybe the idea of giving, even if only a smile on a beautiful day, could make his life begin to turn around. Raymond's stomach was full now. And, somehow, so was his heart!

SO, THEREFORE, WHAT?

Having considered all the above, it seems clear that God's primary action and attitude is one not of wrath but immediate, intense, faithful, and committed love. When we hear about only the wrath of God, we are likely to treat each other in negative ways. We may be unforgiving or, at least, less than loving in our relationships. It does appear that, in many cases, in our modern times, we are hearing more about God's love than God's wrath. But considering the profound love that we learn God has for us, we need to attempt to do likewise and love one another. Here are a few passages to consider about God's love:

> "I have loved [*ahav*] you with an everlasting love [*ahav*]. Therefore, I have continued my faithfulness to you" (Jer 31:3b).

> "But now thus says the Lord, he who created you, O Jacob, he who formed you, O Israel. Do not fear for I have redeemed you. I have called you by name, you are mine . . . you are precious in my sight and honored, and I love ['*ahev*] you" (Isa 43:1, 4).

> "How precious is your steadfast love [*hesed*], O God! All people may take refuge in the shadow of your wings" (Ps 36:7).

"For the mountains may depart and the hills be removed, but my steadfast love [*hesed*] shall not depart from you" (Isa 54:10a).

"The steadfast love [*hesed*] of the Lord never ceases.

His mercies never come to an end" (Lam 3:22).

The many uses of the different words for love in the biblical text show us clearly that love is the theme throughout. God loved us from the beginning, loves us through our lives, and loves us to the end of time. God's anger when we disobey or go astray is assuaged, and we are forgiven and always given another chance. As mentioned above, when the Hebrew word *hesed* is used, this denotes that God is giving us a kind of love or steadfast love when we need it the most and because God can do this, and help us when we cannot help ourselves. When we understand the nuances of the other words for love from the Hebrew, especially *hesed* love, we can come to a deeper understanding of the profound love our God offers to us every day.

CHAPTER 6

Wholeness

THE QUESTION: WHAT IF GOD SEES US EACH AS UNDIVIDED?

What if we could truly recognize ourselves less as being made up of separate parts—body and soul, or body, soul, and spirit—and more as a whole? We even tend to think of soul and spirit separately, although neither are exactly easy to describe, soul and spirit not being visible to the naked eye. But the Hebrew word too often translated into English as "soul" is one that means our "whole being." That word is נֶפֶשׁ (*nép̄eš*—pronounced *nephesh*),[1] and it is a word that encompasses all that we are, including body, soul, and spirit. Ancient Hebrews viewed humans as being one complete entity, rather than being comprised of separate parts. For this reason, the very popular biblical translation "soul" is never really an entirely appropriate translation in the Hebrew Bible. Robert Alter puts it this way: "The number of times it [the word *nephesh*] is still rendered as 'soul' is disconcerting. It's as if the translators felt that you can't really have a Bible without a 'soul.'"[2]

---

1 BDB 659a.

2 Alter, *Art of Bible Translation*, 48.

My "whole being" means all of me: body, mind, spirit; the very essence of who I am that cannot be separated. Might translating the word, at least when employed in Hebrew scripture / Old Testament, back into English as "whole being" instead of *soul* not constitute particularly good news, especially for modern people who may be feeling fragmented and disconnected?

LOOKING AT THE TEXT

The first appearance of the term *nephesh* is found early in the Hebrew Bible. Genesis 2:7 says, "Then the Lord God formed man from the dust of the ground and breathed into his nostrils the breath of life: and the man became *a living being*" (NRSVue). The KJV translated it as "man became *a living soul*."

Psalm 103, in translation, gives a variety of words for *nephesh*, as shown below.

Verse 1, "*Barachi Hashem O nepheshi*," translates as "Bless the Lord, O my *soul*. All that is within me, bless his holy name" (NRSV).

The LB translates this line as "I Bless the holy name of God with all my *heart*."

The CEB says, "Let my whole being bless the Lord. Let *everything inside me* bless his holy name."

Interestingly, MSG renders this verse as "O my *soul*, bless God. *From head to toe*, I'll bless his holy name."

The EASY says, "I say to myself, 'Praise the Lord. *Everything that is in me* bless his holy name.'"

Psalm 103 offers a perfect example of the meaning of the word *nephesh*, which we too often translate as "soul." The reason is that, in Hebrew poetry, as discussed earlier, phrases are not intended to rhyme. Rather, there will often be two matching phrases—phrases that constitute two different ways of saying approximately the same thing. Therefore, in this example, "my soul" and "all that is within me" mean pretty much the same thing.

The concept of an immortal soul that is separate from the body appeared in Judaism only after the return from the Babylonian exile. These ideas were the result of Judaism's interaction with philosophies that were Persian and Hellenistic. In ancient Greece, Plato considered the soul as consisting of reason, spirit, and appetite. The Hebrew word *nephesh*, used later for *soul*, means something like "that which breathes," "the inner being of a human," "a living being," "life," "self," "person," "desire," "appetite," "emotion," and "passion."[3] The description adds that "the *nephesh* becomes a living being by God's breathing into the nostrils" (Gen 2:7). The Septuagint (Hebrew scripture in Greek) and the New Testament often translate this word (*psuche* in Greek) as meaning "the seat of feelings, desires, affections, and aversions." It can be translated as "soul," "life," "self," "breath," or "vital force."

By the time of the writing of the New Testament, the Greek concept of humans as consisting of three parts—body, mind, and spirit or soul—had begun to be accepted. Such are suggested by the apostle Paul, who is influenced by both Hebrew and Greek concepts. He says, for example, at 1 Thessalonians 5:23, probably one of Paul's earliest letters, "May your spirit and soul and body be kept sound and blameless at the coming of our Lord Jesus Christ."

It is understandable that, at least in our culture today and in our time, many (or perhaps even most) Christians tend to think about death as the time the body comes to a permanent end, followed by the disposal of the body by cremation or burial, while the *soul*, being the essence of that person, is believed to ascend to live forever with God. But there are alternate ways to view what happens at death. One could suggest that, because we have been assured in numerous biblical writings that God can create from nothing (*ex nihilo*)[4] whatever or

3 BDB 659b.

4 This concept is attributed to a Jewish text from around 100 BCE in 2 Macca 7:28, which states, "I beg you, my child, to look at the heaven and the earth and see everything that is in them and recognize that God did not make them out of things that existed. And in the same way the human race came into being."

whomever God wishes[5], we may very well have our bodies re-created to live for eternity with God and with those we have loved! It is likely for this reason that the Apostles' Creed clearly proclaims, "I believe in the resurrection of the body."

SCENARIO

Jason had always tried to keep himself "together," but it was getting more and more difficult these days. He had always tended to see himself as being what you might call "scattered." It had not made things easy when his parents got divorced. In order that neither one should be blamed for the fact that the two could not live together, they had made what they were quite sure was the best decision, and that was to basically share their son, Jason. The result was that, from the age of eight, Jason had been required to pack up his little bag every Sunday night and wait at the door for the alternate parent to come and retrieve him. He'd fortunately been able to attend only one school. Still, there was so much his parents could not ever understand. His fellow students seldom chose him to be a close friend because they had soon discovered that their other friends were available most of the time when Jason was only around one week out of every two. Aside from this, as much as his parents loved him and treated him well, they were very different from each other. Consequently, his relationship with each of them was quite different. He tried to simply be himself but too often felt he was adjusting to meet their unspoken needs. Jason, you could say, just felt disjointed far too often. As he was growing to manhood with all the complications that can bring, he found that drugs seemed to calm him but taking them tended to put him in the wrong crowd with people he would not otherwise have chosen.

Jason's mother attended church regularly and had brought him along. He had, to be honest, not paid a lot of attention, and had just

5 For example, at Gen 1:1, God is said to have created the heavens and the earth.

gone with her to be compliant. He had always heard about people having a heart, mind, and spirit. He had heard too about everyone having a soul—and he had been to his uncle's funeral where they said it would be Uncle Chris's soul that would live forever with God in heaven. All this talk had made Jason feel even more disconnected. He had so many questions about this. How many unseen invisible parts did a person actually have? What on earth was the difference between a person's soul and his spirit? If the soul went to heaven when you died, what was it for here on earth? Can you feel it inside you? Jason almost gave up. When he asked the adults about it, they threw up their hands.

Then, one Sunday when Jason was attending a church service with his mom, something caught his attention. The pastor pointed out that the Bible was written in Hebrew and Greek and that what we have are translations. And then he said something that struck Jason very deeply. He said that the Hebrew word *nephesh* doesn't really mean "soul," exactly. It means something more like "whole being." "Wait a minute," Jason thought. "That means 'all of me.' That includes who I am at both of my homes. That means—inside and out, parts that are visible and parts invisible—all of me is loved by God." Suddenly, at that moment, Jason could feel himself coming together. Everything that he was, as the Bible was saying, was one! He asked the pastor if they could talk about this more sometime. The pastor was pleased to have been heard, especially by a young person in the congregation.

They got together the next week, and Jason found he was able to chat with the pastor about how disconnected his life had felt—even though he knew he was loved. The pastor helped him to find a counselor to help him with his issues. And Jason was also able to connect with a young people's group at the church. It turned out two of the kids he already knew from school were part of this group. In time, Jason realized that there were no drugs that would make him feel whole. And he continued to be amazed at how one little word in a foreign ancient language—*nephesh*—had helped him to find his way in this world. Whichever house he was in that week, with his mom or with his dad, Jason knew he was one whole person, and that person was loved by God.

SO, THEREFORE, WHAT?

If we can see ourselves and others each as unified beings that include the very essence of heart, mind, body, and spirit, it is possible that we may be better able to perceive ourselves as complete and less fragmented, as a *nephesh* or a "whole being." What might the consequences be for our relationship with God and each other? For one thing, there is a general conception that, somehow, the body is, as many of the Christian confessions put it, "in bondage to sin." And there is biblical text to support that idea. Paul, for example, says, "I do not understand my own actions. For I do not do what I want, but I do the very thing I hate . . . it is no longer I who do it, but sin that dwells within me" (Rom 7:15–17). People can tend to separate their body and its behaviors from their thoughts about God, feeling that God would not approve of what they are doing. They push away behaviors they feel are shameful or about which they think they should feel shame. There certainly is a place in life for understanding sin. But it is also unhealthful for us to become separated from our legitimate feelings and to ignore the more physical parts of the gift of life that has been given to us. Seeing places where the Hebrew word *nephesh* is employed in the Bible and coming to an understanding that these occasions are not only speaking of some invisible *soul* that is a nonphysical part of us as humans, but in fact all of us, can perhaps bring about a better understanding of how precious we are as a whole being and perceived as such in the eyes of our God. Once we can begin to see ourselves as being whole, being a *nephesh* as the word is translated correctly in the biblical texts, we should be able to begin putting away any feelings of fragmentation.

In today's world, people too often sense that they are being pulled in every direction and that they find themselves behaving in different ways with different people. Some suffer greatly from this sense of fragmentation to the degree that they begin to experience emotional discomfort and even the beginnings of mental illness. The expression "Pull yourself together" is often spoken without the speaker's offering any kind of way for the recipient to accomplish this. At the very least, a deeper understanding of our human identity as one complete entity, a *whole being*, a *living soul*, a *nephesh*, as known in the biblical texts, may be able to assist us in knowing better who we really are.

CHAPTER 7

Resurrection

THE QUESTION: DOES GOD PROMISE THE RESURRECTION OF THE BODY IN THE HEBREW BIBLE?

Now that we have considered how God sees us as more than just a "soul" but rather treasures and loves us as a "whole being," what do we think, from all we have heard and learned over the years, about resurrection and the afterlife? What does the Bible say about heaven or about life after death? And what, from reading the biblical texts, might God have planned for us when we die? Of course, these are questions that will never be fully answered while we are still living in this world. Still, they are addressed to some degree in the biblical texts.

LOOKING AT THE TEXTS

You may be surprised to learn that Hebrew scripture (Christians' Old Testament) does not speak specifically about resurrection of the dead to eternal life in heaven. Resurrection is, of course, a vital component of the good news of the New Testament. Many people are familiar with a text from Job in the KJV, which is employed in the libretto of the most famous of Handel's oratorios to suggest that there is resurrection. As is so often the case, however, the misunderstanding is one of translation! The passage is translated somewhat inaccurately in the KJV and sung by the soprano in Handel's world-famous oratorio "Messiah." The words from the KJV in the libretto are the following, always sung with great conviction: "And though worms destroy this body, yet in my flesh shall I see God" (Job 19:26). The NRSVue, a more accurate translation from the Hebrew, reads quite differently. The words are: "And after my skin has been thus destroyed, then in my flesh shall I see God." It is generally agreed by scholars that this passage indicates the expectation that God will appear to make things right but is not clear about whether that is to happen before or after death. In the Hebrew Bible and Hebrew language, as will be discussed in chapter eleven, only God can create. There is a different word for the kinds of creations in which humans engage. There is also the recurring theme in theological circles that God can create from nothing (*ex nihilo*—"from nothing"). For example, we read in the Bible about women who cannot conceive giving birth (e.g., three of the four matriarchs: Sarah, Rebekah, and Rachel). This implies that it may also not be a problem for a person whose body has gone down into the grave to be revived, if it be God's will. God created us so God can re-create us.

There are only three occasions in Hebrew Scripture where people who died return to life, but in each of these passages this is to life on Earth. These are found in 1 Kings 17:17–24 when Elijah raises a widow's son, in 2 Kings 4:18–37 when Elisha raises the Shunammite's son, and in 2 Kings 13:21 when a dead man is said to have revived when his body was thrown into the same place as Elisha's bones. The purpose of these stories was to confirm the importance of Elijah and then of Elisha. These were, of course, mortal bodies that, once revived, were still mortal. As mentioned earlier, life after death in a heavenly place is not an element of the Judaism of the Hebrew scripture. Some sects of Judaism did, however, during the time of Jesus, believe in the resurrection of the dead. We can presume that the Pharisees believed in the resurrection of the dead and Sadducees did not (Mark 12:18). But we do not possess written records of these two Jewish groups.

One explicit description of a specific kind of resurrection is found in Ezekiel 37, the story of the Valley of the Dry Bones. The writer is experiencing a vision that could also be described as a dream. He is said to have been brought out *by the spirit* of the Lord into a valley full of bones. He is asked to prophesy to the dry bones and, when he does, breath is seen to come into the bones and then sinews and flesh. This narrative, however, is a dream vision and therefore not speaking about physical death and resurrection, but rather about a people who are suffering and afraid, so therefore they are as if dead. The prophet's task is to revive their spirits and their hopes and, in this way, to proclaim new life to them. And so, for this reason, he is given a vision of the dry bones coming to new life and the mandate to revive them.

The Hebrew scripture offers occasional hints about what may happen at the time of death. For example, Ecclesiastes 12:7 says, "And the dust returns to the earth as it was, and the breath [or spirit] returns to God who gave it." This would infer at least that, at physical death, the essence of our being is returned to God from whence it came.

An afterlife is, at the very least, hinted at in Psalm 49:15, where it says, "But God will ransom my *soul* [*nephesh*—"whole being"] from the power of Sheol, for he will receive me." Sheol is not hell, per se. Sheol is, rather, the abode of the dead. The word can be used to mean either a literal place where dead bodies are placed or some subterranean "land of gloom and deep darkness" (Job 10:21). For this reason, some Bible versions will translate Sheol into meaning "the grave" or "the pit." It is mentioned no less than sixty-six times in the Bible. The earlier section of Psalm 49 is speaking about how both rich and poor, wise and foolish, will all see this place. The main point of this psalm, however, appears to be to admonish the reader not to fear poverty because those with wealth will suffer the same fate as everyone else.

In the Christian scriptures, of course, life after death is specifically promised to those who believe and trust in Jesus as the Son of God. And 1 John 2:2 says that Jesus died for all people—"for the sins of the whole world." Then all would gain eternal life. Details are not offered, however, as to how this will take place and what such a life might be. Our culture has filled in the blanks, and, in many respects, our hopes, dreams, and expectations are built around those. Still, the main point of a Christian afterlife is that the person will be able to rejoice in the presence of the triune God for eternity.

SCENARIO

JoAnna and Lily had been best friends for over thirty-five years. They were like sisters in many ways, having met as young children who were sent out to play. They'd attended school together, served as maids of honor for each other's weddings, and had, over the years, shared family meals and watched over each other's children. But the truth is that they had been growing apart. Lily had continued attending her services and even had periods of up to a year or more when she and her family did not go to church at all. In the meantime, her dear friend JoAnna had begun taking a keen interest in all things "spiritual." And these unorthodox interests had been changing and growing! It was not as if they hadn't both tried to talk about it, but as JoAnna had gone farther and farther afield in her beliefs, Lily had decided she was going to keep with the tried and true. When Christmastimes came, JoAnna took to sending Lily stranger and stranger gifts: crystal rock formations to protect her from evil forces, drawings of a mystical nonexistent "spirit guide," and even coupons for discounts on psychic sessions! Lily felt angry, to be honest, and kept telling her husband, Ray, that she wanted to reciprocate by sending JoAnna crucifixes with bleeding Jesuses or Bible commentaries. But Ray reminded her that her friend of these many years only meant well for her with these unusual gifts and wished to share what she believed were her learnings.

A few years went by, and JoAnna passed away at too young an age. Her memorial service was far from what would have made Lily comfortable. But Lily came in time to realize that God's promises of life after death and resurrection were for sure, and she also believed they were for all people. She also came to understand that we may not have been meant to know too much about the afterlife. Some people were more practical or traditional when it came to issues of faith, but God is always trustworthy and true. Over time, Lily remembered her dear friend JoAnna as, at very least, a seeker of the truth. The belief that she had found the truth would always be between JoAnna and her God. As for Lily, she always remembered JoAnna as a gift to her from God, one who had kept her thinking about the meaning of her life and about the nature of her maker! She had never directly discussed the afterlife with JoAnna, but Lily could only guess that each of them had some kind of perception about heaven—and that they would likely differ in almost every aspect and both be wrong. Still, they would both hope and agree on what counted the most—that it would be a place of unending joy, a place where God was, and a home where loved ones gather. So if that were true, their friendship may not have come to an end after all. Who knows? This life on Earth might just have been the beginning!

SO, THEREFORE, WHAT?

The fact that the Hebrew Bible does not specifically speak about resurrection of the dead to eternal life offers a profound lesson that Christians do not often recognize. This means that all the magnificent history, the worship, and the communication over centuries between the Jewish people and God does not and has never revolved around any kind of guarantee or promise of a future life after death in heaven. Rather, Jewish worship is an outpouring of gratefulness for the life being lived right now, in this world—thankfulness for every breath we take, and love for the Creator who chooses to be in relationship with us. If there is life after death, then that would be wonderful. But while we are here on this earth, we have been afforded the gift of life and the ability to trust that God knows what is best for us. Any life after death may be very real, but it is God's business to handle.

And, yes, we all know that when we die, our bodies, if they are cremated, will turn to ashes, or, over time, if they are buried, will turn to dust. But if we consider our theological learnings seriously, we have been told that God can create or re-create us any time, *ex nihilo* or "from nothing." As will be discussed in chapter twelve, only God can perform the action that in Hebrew is known as *bara* or "create." In the Hebrew language, humans never create. We humans only move things around! So there is really no reason why we should have to believe our so-called soul or spirit must be separated from our body at the time of death. The essence of who we are is not necessarily separated at all. Whether your name is John, Mary, Julio, or Ava, it is all of you that comprises who you are—the essence of you—and that essence is what will be with God in an afterlife.

Christians of the more "orthodox" persuasion will point out that the Apostles' Creed clearly contains the statement "I believe in the resurrection of the body." A creed is a statement of faith. Despite its title, this creed is unlikely to have emanated from Jesus's twelve apostles, but it is in fact quite an early writing, having come out of interrogations about beliefs in the early Roman church and known earlier as the Old Roman Creed. It seemed clear that, because witnesses claimed to have seen Jesus after his death as a living human with a body, the bodies of all the believers would also be raised to glory to be with him in the afterlife.

Eternity in an afterlife is something we, as humans, cannot in any way clearly discern. We simply do not have the information. We only dream dreams and have thoughts about what heaven may be. We have heard and read narratives, but even these are generally emanating from other people's dreams and visions. It is likely that we are simply not intended to know too much. This is, as Christians like to say, a strong element of the *mystery of our faith*. To say we are people of faith simply means we are people of trust. We trust in God and all the rest is up to God.

CHAPTER 8

Embodiment

THE QUESTION: DID GOD EVER HAVE A BODY?

Did God of the biblical text ever have a body, and what would be the consequences for our relationship with God and with each other if God was once perceived as having either a feminine or a masculine body? Even if not a physical body, might texts about God reflect aspects and behaviors that are traditionally considered to be particularly masculine or feminine? And how might we respond if this were the case?

It is very likely that many of us today have never thought of God as having a physical body. Our faith statements and doctrines in modern times assure us that God is a pure spirit. Still, it may be that many of the ways we think about God have been profoundly influenced by earlier perceptions of God, especially as male. So it seems worth our while to at least look at how these concepts may have developed and what residual perceptions may yet linger.[1]

---

1 Portions of this chapter related to male and female aspects of God have been adapted from a paper entitled "Lost in Translation: The Sexuality of God in Hebrew Scripture, the New Testament, and the Qur'an," which I presented initially at the Society of Biblical Literature International Meeting in Salzburg, Austria, July 22, 2022. The paper was later enhanced and accepted for a chapter in a Festschrift in honor of John Tracy Greene. The chapter is titled "Lost in Translation: Gender and Sexuality of God in the Hebrew Bible," ed. Zohar

Biblical passages considered "inappropriate" over the millennia appear to have sometimes been reinterpreted or even changed outright, most often leaving an image of a God who is more like a powerful male warrior than a feminine entity: a loving, gentle, caring agent for good. Very early or alternate translations, at times, can indicate a lot about a God with what may be considered traditionally female attributes of having profound love, compassion, and nurture.

Let's look at a few passages that seem to describe God as male and then others with more female-type descriptions, with examples of and possible reasons for mistranslations into the English versions of our Bibles. We need to keep in mind that the early Hebrew scripture writers were likely to have been deeply influenced by conceptions of the gods of neighboring cultures. They then ascribed the powers of these gods to their God, Yahweh. Descriptions of God as a male warrior and, other times, as having a womb, begetting, birthing, mothering, and engaging in midwifery will be considered, along with reasons why God's image may have been sexualized and the consequences of perceiving God as male.

We can generally presume that Hebrew scripture was written primarily by men and, until the last century, also interpreted and translated by men. It is not surprising, therefore, that God was more likely to be viewed as male, possessing a male body, and that the female-like descriptions of God that do exist were ignored, hidden, overridden, or, at the very least, lost in translation, at times not making their way into the texts at all. Some have since been adapted, changed, or corrected to include or display female aspects. The preference for a male God may not exist, in some cases, in the text itself, but in the way that words have been regularly mistranslated. In Hebrew scripture, certain vital words that describe God in any way other than male seem to have been mistranslated (intentionally or unintentionally) or, at least, over time, their meanings have shifted. Earlier meanings, at times, can shed light on a radically different

---

Hadromi-Allouche, Nirmal Fernando, and Keren Abbou Hershkovitz. Publication forthcoming.

image of God from that of being only a power-wielding male warrior,[2] which many passages do indicate (e.g., "The Lord is a warrior; the Lord is his name" (Exod 15:3).

LOOKING AT THE TEXTS

The texts themselves will give hints, if not proof, that God has been perceived as male in some cases and female in others. History indicates it is possible that a matriarchal type of society preceded patriarchy. The earliest evidence of human religious activity surrounding Israel points to the generalized worship of the goddess (25,000 to 8,000 BCE).[3]

God as Male

God has been described as a warrior in the Hebrew Bible and, as such, is often said to have an "outstretched arm." The expression is found, for example, at Deuteronomy 5:15; 26:8; Psalm 136:12; Jeremiah 32:17; and Ezekiel 20:33–34, where—זְרֹעַ (*zərôa'*) means arm.[4] God's arm appears to be a symbol of redemptive power and just rule (e.g., Exod 6:6; Deut 26.8),[5] representing the powerful arm of a mighty warrior; in iconography often holding an arrow or spear, or bolt of lightning (all of which have also been perceived at times as phallic symbols); and in preparation for battle. This would mean

2 Andreas Wagner, *God's Body: The Anthropomorphic God in the Old Testament, trans. Marion Salzmann* (London: T&T Clark, 2019), 14–15. Wagner speaks of idols in Palestine in the late Bronze and Iron Ages, saying "if the armed right arm was raised . . . this posture signaled sovereignty and predominance."

3 LaCocque, *Feminine Unconventional*, 10.

4 Deut 4:34; 5:15; 7:19; 9:29; 11:2; 26:8; 1 Kgs 8:42; 2 Kgs 17:36; 2 Chr 6:32; Ps 136:12; Jer 32:17, 21; Ezek 20:33–34.

5 James Hoffmeier, "The Arm of God Versus the Arm of Pharoah in the Exodus Narratives," *Biblica* 67, no. 3, (1986): 378–87, https://www.jstor.org/stable/42611033. The concept of Pharoah having a conquering arm was already known in Canaan by the 15th century BCE.

that the ancient and well-used term זְרוֹעַ נְטוּיָה (*zərôaʿ nəûyâ*), or "outstretched arm" (e.g., Exod 6:6; Deut 4:34; 5:15; 9:29; 11:2; 26:8), signifies readiness to protect from enemies.[6] It had been a sign of Pharaoh's power,[7] deriving from Egyptian myths about their gods who were worshipped for their physical ability to protect in times of war. The Egyptian Pharaoh was viewed as the god Horus incarnate—a god who waged war but who was also believed to be responsible for fertility. The sexual acts of the Egyptian gods had been, during the period 2900–2100 BCE,[8] (at least ritually) reenacted by the kings of Egypt to ensure fertility and crop growth.[9] Language related to Pharoah's conquering arm begins to appear around the period of the Middle Kingdom (1970–1800 BCE).[10] A warrior with an outstretched arm would have been a familiar depiction of a god, one the writers of Exodus and Deuteronomy then later engaged, but by then ascribing this power to their God, Yahweh, presumably in battle.

The Hebrew word זְרוֹעַ (*zərôaʿ*), meaning "arm," consists of the identical three consonants ע, ר, and ז, which also comprise the word for seed, semen, and sperm.[11] God's outstretched arm or זְרוֹעַ נְטוּיָה (*zərôaʿ nəûyâ*) suggests physical might but also, at the very least, could imply fertility. This outstretched arm can, of course, represent a warrior's spear-wielding arm with the purpose of protecting the people in war, but equally as an erect arm stretched out to spread seed and, thereby, represent fertility. At Isaiah 61:11, a phrase is engaged using the word זֵרוּעֶיהָ (*zêrūʿehā*), meaning "that which is sown." It indicates the bringing forth of life that God can make

6 BDB 639b, 282–83.

7 Wagner, *God's Body*, 104.

8 Pirjo Lapinkivi, "The Sumerian Sacred Marriage and Its Aftermath in Later Sources," in *Sacred Marriages: The Divine-Human Sexual Metaphor from Sumer to Early Christianity*, ed. Martti Nissinen and Risto Uro (Ann Arbor, MI: Eisenbrauns, 2008), 7, https://doi.org/10.5325/j.ctv1bxgzv8.4.

9 Henri Frankfort, *Kingship and the Gods: A Study of Near Eastern Religion as the Integration of Society and Nature* (1948; repr., Chicago: University of Chicago Press, 1978), 188.

10 Hoffmeier, "Arm of God," 380.

11 BDB 282–83.

happen. The term *outstretched arm* spoke of God's power and ability to protect. The Egyptian gods' sign of power in warfare and also, perhaps, even their fertility have been appropriated and assigned to Yahweh in the use of this term. The writers of Hebrew scripture appear to have been engaging the Egyptians' own well-known terminology in relation to power, now to render them powerless,[12] at least according to the texts.

People in surrounding cultures in the ancient world worshipped both male and female gods. Many gods were represented as having male bodies or even with images of single male body parts. For example, an erect male organ was displayed in processions in honor of the god Dionysus, originally a god of fertility.[13] Statues of individual erect phalluses can still be seen today in Delos, Greece, at Stoivadeion, a temple to Dionysus. Statues with or of erect phalluses appear to have represented fertility, virility, life force, and generative power, and they were known in ancient Greece from the seventh millennium BCE. These included statues of Hermes, son of the god Zeus in the Greek Pantheon, as well as those honoring Dionysus. In Egypt, Osiris was worshipped as a god of fertility and also as the embodiment of the dead and resurrected king.[14] From the fourth millennium BCE, the god Min, son of Isis and Osiris, was worshipped as a fertility god. In statuary, Min displays a fully erect phallus.[15] In Ugaritic texts, Ba'al was a storm and fertility god.[16] The Hebrew Bible emerged within an environment of surrounding cultures. There seems little doubt that

---

12 Hoffmeier, "Arm of God," 387.

13 Carl Kerenyi, *Archetypical Image of Indestructible Life* (Princeton, NJ: Princeton University Press, 1976), 273–388.

14 G. D. Hornblower, "Osiris and the Fertility Rite," *Man* 41, no. 71 (1941), 94–103, https://doi.org/10.2307/2792421.

15 Stephanie Lynn Budin, "Phallic Fertility in the Ancient Near East and Egypt," in *Reproduction: From Antiquity to the Present Day*, ed. Nick Hopwood, Rebecca Flemming, and Lauren Kassell (Cambridge University Press, 2018), https://doi.org/10.1017/9781107705647.006.

16 Frank Moore Cross, *Canaanite Myth and Hebrew Epic: Essays in the History of the Religion of Israel* (Cambridge, MA: Harvard University Press, 1997), 147.

its writers would have appropriated, adapted, and rewritten certain religious concepts they encountered, as they presented the people of Israel with both a written "history" and direction.[17] This movement into their future now focused on Yahweh, the God who would be protecting and parenting and who commanded complete loyalty.[18] The attitudes about God being male and having a body appear to have emerged and developed in Israel out of this milieu.

God as Male with a Consort

In the Hebrew Bible, a female consort is at least hinted at for God. Having such a consort would assume Yahweh to have been viewed as male. Asherah (or *asherah*, the symbol of which is a pole) is mentioned at 1 Kings 14:15 and 23 and 2 Kings 17:10 but is always presented in the Bible as an abomination to be marginalized and removed.[19] A "queen of heaven" is inferred at Jeremiah 7:18 and named at 44:17–25, but her worship is only said to be angering God. Still, such a presence, albeit mentioned only in the negative, speaks of an earlier possible belief in and worship of her. Collections of ancient Hebrew inscriptions were unearthed in the 1960s and 1970s, and they appear to confirm that Yahweh was believed to have had a female consort, Asherah.[20] J. A. Emerton suggests, rather, a grammatical approach should be taken, and he concludes that these texts should not read "Yahweh and his Asherah" but rather "Yahweh and his *asherah*," indicating that they refer not to the goddess Asherah but

---

17 Frevel, *History of Ancient Israel*, 8.

18 Herbert Niehr, "The Rise of YHWH in Judahite and Israelite Religion: Methodological and Religio-Historical Aspects," in *The Triumph of Elohim: From Yahwishms to Judaisms*, ed. Diana Vikander Edelman (Leuven, Belgium: Peeters, 1995; Grand Rapids, MI: Eerdmans, 1995), 71. Citations refer to the Eerdmans edition; and Othmar Keel and Christoph Uehlinger, *Gods, Goddesses, and Images of Ancient Israel* (Minneapolis: Fortress Press, 1998), 177, 210, 385.

19 Francesca Stavrakopoulou, *God: An Anatomy* (New York: Alfred A. Knopf, 2022), 153.

20 Stavrakopoulou, *God: An Anatomy*, 151.

to some kind of image that is her symbol.[21] The Jeremiah texts listed above make it clear that God is greatly displeased with the people's having led and participated in a ritual of worship that included the presentations of cakes and libations to a female queen of heaven. These texts suggest that, in ancient Israel, there had been at least some worship of a female deity or consort of Yahweh, which was later stamped out. Susan Ackerman, in her 2022 book *Gods, Goddesses, and the Women Who Serve Them*, states, "I count myself among those scholars, moreover, who claim that Asherah's cult image was being adorned, . . . and therefore, the goddess Asherah was being worshipped . . . in the Jerusalem temple during Josiah's reign because many in ancient Israel . . . understood this goddess to be the consort of the Israelite national God, Yahweh. I have found the inscriptional evidence that comes from the sites of Kuntillet 'Ajrud and khirbet el-Qom to be particularly significant."[22] These include the phrase "Yahweh [of Samaria or of Temen] and his Asherah."

It seems likely that God, who was earlier perceived to be male with a female consort, over time came to embrace aspects of both what are seen as the male and the female, melded into the one androgenous Deity.

Controversy over Female Attributes of God

In recent years, feminist scholars have taken more and more interest in searching out female aspects of God that may have been either repressed or mistranslated.[23] In 2015, however, David J. A. Clines presented a lecture entitled "The Scandal of a Male Bible," claiming strongly that "there are no descriptions whatever in the Hebrew Bible

---

21 J. A. Emerton, "Yahweh and His Asherah: The Goddess or Her Symbols?" *Vetus Testamentum* 49, no. 3 (1999): 315–37, https://doi.org/10.1163/156853399774228010.

22 Susan Ackerman, *Gods, Goddesses, and the Women Who Serve Them* (Grand Rapids, MI: Eerdmans, 2022), 210.

23 Elizabeth Schussler Fiorenza, Phyllis Trible, Gale A. Yee, Phyllis Bird, and Mary Daly, to name a few.

of God as a female."[24] Alastair Haines disagreed and responded with "The Masculine Language of the Bible: A Response to David Clines."[25] In it, Haines disagreed with Clines's conclusions, pointing out that too often, masculinity has been conflated with virtue. Clines offered a subsequent article in response, "Alleged Female Language about the Deity in the Hebrew Bible."[26] And in a later article entitled "The Most High Male: Divine Masculinity in the Bible," Clines pronounced yet again, "There is not a single instance of female language about the deity in the Hebrew Bible, that is, of language suggesting that the deity is viewed as female, whether as a mother or a midwife, or in any other typical female activity."[27] In 2022, Hanne Loland Levinson offered a reply with her article "Still Invisible after All These Years? Female God-Language in the Hebrew Bible: A Response to David J. A. Clines."[28] In it, Levinson correctly pointed to what she saw as Clines's three methodological problems: selective choice of conversation partners; inattention to the history of feminist biblical scholarship, such as excluding metaphor theory;[29] and his not clearly defining

24 David J. A. Clines, "The Scandal of a Male Bible" (Ethel M. Wood Lecture at King's College London, London, UK, April 30, 2015), 2, https://www.academia.edu/10977758/The_Scandal_of_a_Male_Bible.

25 Alastair Haines, *"The Masculine Language of the Bible: A Response to David Clines," New Male Studies: An International Journal* 5, no. 1 (2016): 5–30, https://www.academia.edu/20633158/The_masculine_language_of_the_Bible_A_response_to_David_Clines.

26 David J. A. Clines, "Alleged Female Language about the Deity in the Hebrew Bible," *JBL* 140, no. 2 (2021), 229–49, https://doi.org/10.15699/jbl.1402.2021.1.

27 David J. A. Clines, "The Most High Male: Divine Masculinity in the Bible," paper delivered at the Feminist Interpretations section of the Society of Biblical Literature International Meeting, Buenos Aires, Argentina, July 22, 2015, www.academia.edu/14079928.

28 Hanne Loland Levinson, "Still Invisible after All These Years? Female God-Language in the Hebrew Bible: A Response to David J. A. Clines," *JBL* 141, no. 2 (2022), https://doi.org/10.15699/jbl.1412.2022.1.

29 Sallie McFague, in her book entitled *Metaphorical Theology: Models of God in Religious Language*, points out that religious language is largely metaphorical and needs to be understood this way. (Philadelphia: Fortress Press, 1982), 193.

what "female" language means in relation to God. This very active scholarly interaction leaves us with little doubt that the issue of God's gender in the Hebrew Bible remains a lively and current topic. The second item in Levinson's list, recognizing and accepting the use of metaphor in relation to God,[30] seems important. If indeed God does not possess a physical body, clearly then everything in scripture referring to God's body and behavior, male or female, as well as living things to which God is compared, comprises metaphor.[31]

El Shaddai: Male "God Almighty" or Female "God with Breasts?"

In the Hebrew Bible, El Shaddai is one powerful and seemingly male name for God (e.g., Genesis 17:1, "I am God Almighty [El Shaddai]; walk before me, and be blameless," and Genesis 35:11, "I am God Almighty [El Shaddai]: be fruitful and multiply"). The terms here are אל שדי (*ēl šadday*), or El Shaddai, and שַׁדַּי (*šadday*),[32] or Shaddai, in Genesis 49:25: "By the God of your father, who will help you, by the Almighty, who will bless you." Most importantly, in the six times Genesis mentions the name Shaddai no less than five are in relation to fertility blessings.[33] Genesis 17:01 states that the people will be made to be "exceedingly numerous." Genesis 28:03, 35:11, and 48:03 state that El Shaddai will make you "fruitful and numerous." And, to the point, Genesis 49:25 includes what appears to be a deliberate poetic play on pairing words, balancing the word El Shaddai with the phrase "the blessings of the breasts and of the womb."[34] As discussed in chapter

30 Janet Martin Soskice, *Metaphor and Religious Language* (Oxford: Clarendon Press, 1985).

31 Christl M. Maier, *Daughter Zion, Mother Zion: Gender, Space, and the Sacred in Ancient Israel* (Minneapolis: Fortress Press, 2008), 17–21. Metaphor and new theories of metaphor are examined at length here.

32 BDB 995a.

33 David Biale, "The God with Breasts: El Shaddai in the Bible," *History of Religions* 21, no. 3 (1982), 247, doi.org/10.1515/9781503634350-003.

34 Howard Eilberg-Schwartz, *God's Phallus and Other Problems for Men and Monotheism* (Boston: Beacon Press, 1995), 115.

one, Hebrew poetry regularly consists of parallelisms in which similar but different words are matched between two lines of text. This form of poetry appears to have the purpose of providing an opportunity for the reader to experience two similar ways of looking at something. It shows how no individual word or description can be all-encompassing. For this reason, it is poetically particularly significant that the term El Shaddai is matched up five times with "breasts and womb."[35]

The word El Shaddai (traditionally translated as "God Almighty") has a lengthy history of translations, including *omnipotent* in the Vulgate and *self-sufficient* in the Midrashic works. The word Shaddai also was said to relate the concept of a mountain god, from the Akkadian word *shadu*, but there is no obvious mountain in the Egyptians' story.[36] Then, later, a god of the plains was suggested, but again with no obvious related location.[37] David Biale's article "The God with Breasts: El Shaddai in the Bible"[38] covers possible meanings and usage of the term from as early as the tenth century BCE onward. In Genesis, El Shaddai is only mentioned in relation to the patriarchs. Biale noted that, back in 1964, E. A. Speiser had concluded that "the jury is still out on the original meaning of El Shaddai," pointing out that this still seemed to be the case.[39] The earliest known meanings of such words can be carefully studied but, importantly, it is vital to remember that the biblical authors who used them may themselves have had no idea of their origins. The word

---

35 Robert Alter, "The Dynamics of Parallelism," in *The Art of Biblical Poetry*, rev. ed. (New York: Basic Books, 2011).

36 Friedrich Delitzsch, *Prolegomena eines neuen hebräisch-arämaischen Wörterbuchs zum Alten Testament* (Leipzig: J. C. Hinrichs, 1886), 95–97; Friedrich Delitzsch, *Assyrisches Handworterbuch* (Leipzig: J. C. Hinrichs, 1896), 960, 642; and William F. Albright, "The Names Shaddai and Abram," *JBL* 54, no. 4 (1935), 180–93, https://doi.org/10.2307/3259784.

37 Manfred Weippert, "Erwangungen zur Etymologie des Gottesnamens 'El Shaddai'," in *Zeitschrift der Deutischen Morgenlandischen Gesellschaft issue* 111 no. 36 (1961), 42–62.

38 Biale, "God with Breasts."

39 Biale, "God with Breasts," 242. Here, he quotes E. A. Speiser, *Genesis*, Anchor Bible (Garden City, NY: Doubleday, 1964), 124.

Shaddai suggests the word may have derived from the Hebrew word שַׁד (*šd*), which means "female breasts."[40] El Shaddai would translate to something like "breasted God" or "God with breasts." If the word, indeed, is connected to breasts, then the name El Shaddai could have earlier been connected in some way with the compassion or רחמים- (*rachamim*) of God, which is formally the same word as *womb*, this meaning later being lost.

According to the biblical text, following his experience at the burning bush, Moses is said to ask God's name. God's response of יהוה (Yahweh) at Exodus 3:14 is untranslatable but has been described by translators as something like "I am what I am" without proper noun naming, and therefore beyond any concept of gender.[41] Exodus 6:2–3, however, suggests that El Shaddai may have been an older known name for a god who had been worshipped, and the people are now told this name was to be put aside for reasons that are not clarified—that the name Yahweh for God was to be known from that point forward. It says, in the NRSVue, "God [Elohim] also spoke to Moses and said to him: 'I am the Lord [Yahweh],'" which is, of course, a nongendered proper noun. "I appeared to Abraham, Isaac, and Jacob as *God Almighty* [El Shaddai or possibly "God with breasts"] but by my name '*the Lord* [Yahweh] I did not make myself known to them."[42] It seems consequential that the Israelites, at least according to the biblical narrative, were in a time of transition and clearly being directed to put away their previous names for and concepts of God. They are now to perceive their deity in a different way as they move forward as a people, according to the story.

As neither of the two names (Yahweh and Shaddai) is specifically male, it is possible that God had been known by the ancient breasted god's title and now the people were directed to put their older concepts of God away and to worship Yahweh, the god who has no gender

40 BDB 994b.

41 Moore Cross, *Canaanite Myth*, 61.

42 Notice here how English translations make the issue of the different meanings almost indiscernible!

and no name other than something like "I am what I am." In later passages, (e.g., Numbers 24:16; Ruth 1:20; Isaiah 13:6; Ezekiel 1:24; Joel 1:15; and thirty-one times in Job), however, any connection with a possible breast-related meaning of the word Shaddai seems to have been lost. There is evidence that the name that connected God with breasts could be, at least, one earlier meaning of the term—one that may have reflected ancient agrarian societies or possibly even mother goddess worship. If it did mean "breasts," such a name could imply a nurture, protection, and safety that can only be found in the kind of trusting innocence, as at a mother's breast.

The Hebrew Bible's writers, as previously mentioned, influenced by surrounding Near Eastern cultures, appear to have adapted some concepts familiar to the people while changing others with the purpose of creating a new written "history" story for Israel that would be acceptable to those who were to receive it.[43] There exists a late eighth-century BCE clay figurine of a woman with heavy breasts, excavated in Jerusalem among hundreds of others from houses and tombs.[44] Such female iconography goes back much further; for example, there is a "figurine fragment from twelfth century BCE Shechem . . . [that] shows the breasted Egyptian goddess Isis and the infant god Horus" at her breast.[45] The concept of a deity with breasts who influences fertility should, therefore, not be surprising at the time of the writings of Genesis and Exodus. In the biblical narrative about the Hebrews coming out of Egypt,[46] there would seem perhaps to have arisen a need for a different concept of God, one whose main and most-needed attribute would no longer be related to fertility or motherly nurture as breasts could provide but rather strong military-type protection.

The following are translations of El Shaddai:

---

43 Frevel, *History of Ancient Israel*, 8.

44 Stavrakopoulou, *God: An Anatomy*, 272, fig. 36.

45 Stavrakopoulou, *God: An Anatomy*, 272.

46 Niehr, "Rise of YHWH," 47. Niehr says, "The Hebrew Bible does not depict the histories of Judah and Israel as they took place, but as they have been reimagined in the mind of the writers."

> "I appeared to Abraham, Isaac, and Jacob, as **God Almighty**, but by my name **The Lord** I did not make myself fully known to them" (Exodus 6:3 NRSVue).

> "I appeared to Abraham, Isaac, and Jacob as **El Shaddai**, but by my name **Yahweh** I did not make myself known to them" (my direct translation).

Most interestingly, God's name is proclaimed to have been El Shaddai but later Yahweh. As discussed above, El Shaddai may have in ancient times meant "breasted God," connected with fertility blessings.[47] God's activities at times—such as midwifery, birthing, and nursing—were associated with females, but they were also described in masculine terms such as being a protector and warrior.

God Giving Birth or Begetting

The status of a mother consisting of preservation, growth, and social acceptance is an ideal employed by the authors of the Hebrew Bible to describe divine activity. Claudia D. Bergmann speaks of "the narratives of the delayed or difficult conception of the ancestors of Israel," pointing out that narratives of Genesis show how divine influence ensures the early growth of the people.[48] So it is not surprising that throughout these narratives in the Hebrew Bible, God is, at times, described in female terms.

Mistranslations or, at least, unclear translations often occur in texts that discuss God as *birthing* and *begetting*. Deuteronomy 32:18 states, "You were unmindful of the rock that bore you [or begot you]. You forgot the God who gave you birth" (NRSVue). Here are a few examples of the wide variety of translations of this

47 Doreen M. McFarlane, "Lost in Translation: Gender and Sexuality of God in the Hebrew Bible," in *Scriptural Sexualities*, ed. Zohar Hadromi-Allouche, Nirmal Fernando, and Keren Abbou Hershkovitz. Publication forthcoming.

48 Claudia D. Bergmann, "Mothers of a Nation: How Motherhood and Religion Intermingle in the Hebrew Bible," *Open Theology* 6, no. 1 (2020), 142, https://doi.org/10.1515/opth-2020-0012.

text: "begat . . . formed" (KJV), "fathered—gave you birth" (NIV), "bore you . . . gave you birth" (NRSV, NRSVue), "gave you life . . . brought you into the world" (MSG). This text presumes that the rock is God, metaphorically giving birth to (female image) or siring (male image) the nation of Israel.[49] The word ילד (*yld*) here, as in other biblical texts, could be translated as "to bear or give birth." But this same word is often translated to English as "beget," which most often indicates the male's emission of semen to create new life (e.g., Gen 17:20; Lev 25:45; 2 Kgs 20:18; Isa 45:10; Jer 16:3; Ezek 18:14).[50]

It is helpful to consider the English words for the action that only a female can do of "birthing or giving birth" as opposed to the word *beget*, generally employed to describe the male action of breeding, siring, generating, or causing a child to be created. The *Oxford English Dictionary* (*OED*) says that *to beget* means (especially of a man) "to bring [a child] into existence by the process of reproduction."[51] Isaiah 66:9 employs this same verb, ילד (*yld*), twice. In this case, the verb suggests giving birth but possibly even God in the role of a midwife (discussed below). "Shall I open the womb and not deliver [אוֹלִיד (*'ôlîd*)]?" "Shall I, the one who delivers [הַמּוֹלִיד (*hammôlîd*)], shut the womb? says your God."

At Isaiah 42:13, God is described as behaving like a warrior who cries out and shouts against his enemies. Then, at 42:14, God is said to be crying out, but this time gasping and panting like a woman in labor. Such a text is not making God female, but the two verses appear to describe God in first a male way, then followed by a female type of action: demonstrating first a deliberate act of a warrior, followed by a nondeliberate act of crying out, as if from birthing pains. We are reminded that male warrior activity is, at least to some extent, one of choice, while birthing is a natural event over which females have little or no control.

---

49 Maier, *Daughter Zion*, 19.

50 In English, the word *begat* is most often used for action of the male.

51 *OED*, 2nd ed., vol. 7 (Oxford: Oxford University Press, 1819), s.v. "beget."

God's birthing or begetting a son is also suggested at Psalm 2:7, which states, "He said to me 'You are my son. Today I have begotten [יְלִדְתִּיךָ (*yəlidtîkā*)] you'." As discussed earlier, the concept of a god siring a king was also present in the myths of earlier neighboring cultures, including the myths of Egyptian gods.[52]

God with a Womb

In relation to carrying a child within the body, there are two different words for womb in Hebrew. One is רַחַם (*rāḥam*) or "womb" (grammatically masculine), described in the BDB as related to the word *compassion*[53] and found at Genesis 49:25 in the "blessings of the breasts and of the womb," and another, בִּטְנִי (*biṭnî*) (grammatically feminine), described in the BDB as "belly, body, or womb."[54] This word is found at Job 3:10b—"because it did not shut the doors of my [mother's] womb"—and Job 38:29—"From whose womb does the ice come forth and who has given birth to the hoarfrost of heaven?" The answer to this question clearly seems to be God. Isaiah 46:3 engages both words in poetic language. The purpose of the use of matching but different phrases in Hebrew poetry, as discussed earlier, appears to be to say the same thing in two different ways while allowing breathing space for interpretation so the biblical text does not become inflexible.[55] The NRSVue translation does not clarify. In it, God is saying "[you] who have been borne *by me* [Hebrew text does not say "by me"] from your birth, carried from the womb." Here, to clarify the poetic use of the two matching words, is a more direct translation: "who are borne from the belly [בֶּטֶן(*beṭen*)] who are lifted from the *womb* [רַחַם (*rāḥam*)]" (translation mine). To be lifted from the womb sounds more like the act of a midwife than of the birthing

52 Moore Cross, *Canaanite Myth*, 147; Niehr, "Rise of YHWH," 71; and Keel and Uehlinger, *Gods, Goddesses, and Images*, 177, 210, 385.

53 BDB 933a.

54 BDB 105b.

55 Alter, Robert, chapter one, "The Dynamics of Parallelism" in *The Art of Biblical Poetry*, NY: Basic Books (2011), 21–28.

mother. Either way, it is describing the closeness and care of God at the sometimes very perilous times of birth. At Jeremiah 1:4, it is made clear that God not only created the human (the prophet in this case) but knew the prophet even before he was formed in the womb!

God Acting as a Midwife

Midwives appear in a few biblical narratives (e.g., Gen 35:17; 38:28; Exod 1:15–21). God is described as engaging in midwifery at Psalm 22:9a and 71:6 and also in opening the wombs of Leah (Gen 29:31) and of Rachel (Gen 30:22). As midwifery was and is virtually always a woman's profession,[56] it seems clear that God is being described in this role generally taken by women. In this regard, Psalm 22:9a says, "Yet it was you who took [גֹחִי (*Gohi*)][57] me from the womb," and Psalm 71:6b states, "It was you who took me [גוֹזִי (*gaze*)][58] from my mother's womb." Job 10:18a says, "Why did you bring me forth [הֹצֵאתָנִי (*hōṣēʾtānî*)][59] from the womb?"

Clines contends that God is not being described as a midwife in Psalm 71:6 because the verb has been changed (in English?) from one that means "to cut" to a verb that means "to take out."[60] The verb, indeed, means "to cut or sever,"[61] but to grab hold of a baby who is emerging from the womb does require the cutting or severing of the umbilical cord in order to separate the child from the body of the mother. This is the work of a midwife, whose primary job is to assist in what is a natural process, so, here, God is depicted as a midwife.

Important here is another aspect of mistranslation! The actual text of Psalm 71:6 translates into English as "You took me [or severed me]

---

56 Shalvi/Hyman Encyclopedia of Jewish Women, s.v. "Midwife: Bible," by Carol Meyers, last modified June 23, 2021, https://jwa.org/encyclopedia/article/midwife-bible.

57 BDB 160b.

58 BDB 159a.

59 BDB 422a.

60 Clines, "Alleged Female Language," 7.

61 BDB 159a.

from my mother's womb." There is no indication of gender in relation to God, as it says "you." Yet many English translations translate this as "*He* took me out of my mother's womb" (e.g., "Thou art *he* that took me out of my mother's bowels" (KJV), "You are *he* who took me from my mother's womb" (ESV), "You are *he* who took me out of my mother's womb" (NKJV), and "You are *he* who took me from my mother's womb" (NKJV, NASB, ASV, JPS—Tanakh 1917, WEB). The choice of this mistranslation of "sever" or "cut," and especially of the term *he* in the place of *you*, indicates that the translators could not comprehend God as being anything other than male. Even though the term *he* is not present in the text, as seen above, it is employed in many translations.

Clines is correct, of course, in saying that the opening and closing of wombs does not make God female. He is economical with the truth, however, when he does not say clearly that God is depicted as playing the role of a midwife, exclusively a woman's task at the time. It is an academic leap from that statement to his saying "The deity can do this because he is a powerful male god."[62] The God of the Bible is powerful and may appear to be a powerful male in many instances, but the opening and closing of wombs has nothing to do with God's being male. Although Clines points out that "there is nothing female about his control of women's fertility,"[63] he fails to say, "but neither is there anything male about it."[64]

In postbiblical writings, a Midrashic passage in the Babylonian Talmud (*Sotah* 11b) reflects on the work of God in the role of a midwife. In the story, a heavenly messenger (often a euphemism for God)[65] takes on the duties of a midwife, washing the newborn. When the Hebrews are freed from Pharaoh's power, they praise God whom they

62 Clines, "Alleged Female Language," 3.

63 Clines, "Alleged Female Language," 3.

64 Comments will be refrained from about how males too often have tried to control women's fertility.

65 At Gen 16:13, Hagar proclaims, after seeing the angel, that she has truly "seen the one who sees me" (NIV).

say has encouraged conception, assisted with delivery, and protected each childbearing mother.[66]

God as a Mother

One passage that describes God as a mother or as being mother-like is Numbers 11:12. Here, Moses complains to God, saying "Did I conceive all this people? Did I give birth to them, that you should say to me 'Carry them in your bosom, as a wet nurse[67] carries a nursing child . . . ?" Moses's complaining that he is not the parent does not directly make God the parent, but it is implied, at least, that Moses sees God in that role. The strangest words in English translation here are those of "nursing father" in the KJV. Although dictionaries employ the term הָאֹמֵן (*hāʾōmēn*) as "foster father" or "nurse,"[68] and the word also implies a guardian or one who supports, the English word *to nurse* generally speaks of what only a woman can do; that is, feeding the infant or young child directly with milk from her breast. Clearly, no father can do this, even though a lactating woman who is not the natural mother can do it. That the "nurse" word is present here for God indicates that the text itself attributes God with female-like qualities and behaviors, even though translators have too often found themselves unable or unwilling to make this clear due, it appears, to hegemony.

God is also depicted as behaving like a mother in Hosea 11:3–4, teaching the child to walk, taking the child up in arms, leading the child with cords of human kindness and bands of love, and being to

66 Jane Kanarek, "The Warrior God as Midwife," *Sh'ma: A Journal of Jewish Responsibility,* April 1, 2011, 3–4, http://shma.com.

67 The KJV added the word *father* after "nursing" in this verse, losing the meaning in translation. The conditioning effect that the KJV had, also in the colonial period, by using such interpretations, are yet not unconditioned despite the revisions and new translations. Further, the KJV was translated under many instructions given by King James I; one was to make sure that the translation was in harmony with the theology of the Church of England.

68 BDB 52b.

the child as those who lift infants to their cheeks and bending down to them and feeding them. All of these are traditionally motherly activities. Clines points out that these can be not only the acts of mothers but also of fathers.[69] Still, women of biblical times were tasked with these activities toward children, while men generally appear to have labored outside the home, utilizing other skills.[70] The duties of caring for a household and for children have changed substantially, even over the past hundred years. In biblical times, it seems assured that the amount of physical labor a woman was required to engage in daily would have been time consuming. Giving birth to and caring for children, breastfeeding, cooking, cleaning, and providing for all the home-related family needs were complex and, traditionally, women's work. It seems unlikely that men would have been substantially engaged in these activities.

Summing Up the Possibilities

We have seen that God has been perceived at various times in history as having a physical body: in the Hebrew Bible with arms (the words for arms possibly even denoting a phallus, sometimes erect) and other body parts. God as El Shaddai could signify a powerful male warrior, but this same word may earlier have described God in female anatomical terms such as having nurturing breasts. In Hebrew scripture, God is metaphorically also compared to a woman having a womb, performing the duties of a midwife, acting like a mother: nursing, giving birth to, and nurturing the young. The name of God shifted in time from El Shaddai, which may have had some history of female connotation, to Yahweh, a nongendered and virtually untranslatable proper noun. Due at least in part to mistranslation, intentional or unintentional, the deity in the Hebrew Bible has, nevertheless, been primarily viewed

---

69 Clines, "Alleged Female Language," 11.

70 Tikva Frymer-Kensky, *Motherprayer: The Pregnant Woman's Spiritual Companion* (New York: Riverhead, 1996), xvi.

as male. Translators have demonstrated a strong bias for a male God, and they have too often ignored and passed over very real opportunities to consider at least the acts of God in feminine terms, using the terms God and *he* without even considering Goddess. The problem is in deciding what gender to give the deity. English Bible translations have consistently used the word God, a noun that is at least grammatically masculine.

The plethora of translations that present God as male and "the dark reality of subsequent patriarchal theological interpretations that have depicted God as a dominant male figure that subjects women to male hierarchy" have resulted in profound consequences for women, who have over centuries been marginalized.[71] Over centuries, sermons have depicted a patriarchal God and have accentuated patriarchy. Marriage vows in the past required the woman to vow obedience to her husband. Women have been instructed to stay quiet in worship and have been denied leadership opportunities. They have also been denied voting rights. Royal accession in many countries required the son to take precedence over an older daughter. Church doctrines demanded that only males be ordained. This is all changing but often far too slowly.

It has become recognized in recent decades that, however honorable pastoral and scholarly intentions may have been, we (both male and female) often unwittingly bring our gender-related biases and our own cultural and contemporary assumptions into our translations and our work with scripture. Lena-Sophia Tiemeyer rightly points out that "modern authors are shaped by our present society and thus their interpretations are aligned with what we today deem to be acceptable interpretations of biblical material . . . [and] the

71 Simon Howard, Debra L. Oswald, Mackenzie Kirkman, "The Relationship between God's Gender, Gender System Justification and Sexism," *The International Journal for the Psychology of Religion*, 30, no. 3 (2020): 216–230, http://www.tandfonline.com/toc/hjpr20/curr; and Ally Moder, "Woman, Personhood, and the Male God: A Feminist Critique of Patriarchal Concepts of God in View of Domestic Abuse," *Feminist Theology* 28, no. 1 (2019): 85–103, https://doi.org/10.1177/0966735019859471.

biblical texts thus form vehicles for conveying the modern author's political and religious views."[72]

SCENARIO

No one would ever have described Marian's father as a bad person. He had provided for Marian and her mother all those years! He had paid for Marian's piano lessons when she wanted them. He had never really denied her things she needed. But truth be told, she had always been somewhat afraid of him. When she was a small child, she always found him to be too big and too loud. Dad was also demanding. He held high standards for his little family, and Marian believed she could never meet up to his unreasonable expectations. It was nothing serious, really, but she'd better have her bed made before breakfast, she'd better not leave food on her plate, and she'd better help mother with the dishes and housecleaning. And, of course, she'd better go to Sunday school and church every week and make sure he was proud of her. He'd never hit her or even threatened to do so. It was difficult for her to even discern why she felt so afraid of him. But then, she'd also always been careful not to offend him in any way. And he was never a person she felt she could talk to or tell her troubles. Dad was to be pleased and appeased, and then everything would be all right with the world. Marian had never even tried to test that fact.

Marian was a teenager before she realized that she had somehow been raised with the same feelings about God. She had learned in Sunday school about Jesus being loving and brotherly and kind and gentle. But, probably quite unintentionally on the part of the clergy, she had been given the impression that God was like not only a demanding male and father but like *her* father. God was watching her all the time and expecting her to meet God's standards of good behavior, or else! Or else what? She had no clear concept of this, but she believed

72 Lena-Sophia Tiemeyer, "The Lover and the Friend: The Depiction of Jonathan's Sexuality in Contemporary Literature," in Hadromi-Allouche, Fernando, and Hershkovitz, *Scriptural Sexualities*. Publication forthcoming.

she would be punished if she stepped out of line. She had been given scripture to read that described God as a deity of wrath and anger. She felt deeply that the purpose of both God and her dad was to keep her in line. And, yes, for sure she was afraid of them both. For this unspoken reason, Marian did not really enjoy going to church that much.

As she became an adult, she realized that her dad had lost his grip of power over her. She went off to college and then to work. She began living on her own and, at the same time, her father suffered from some serious illnesses and became quite frail. She started going to a different church closer to where she had moved. This new pastor stressed different aspects of God. Marian gradually learned about God's incredible unending love for her. She got in the habit of Bible reading and found there were several narratives in which God's anger was assuaged, and God would actually be sorry for having even considered punishing his people. Even though, of course, she'd heard it before, Marian came to realize the importance of the Bible teaching how God sent God's only son to die for her and to be raised from the dead, so she could be assured she'd always be forgiven! Now she began to accept what kind of love such a gift could mean. In time, Marian was able to be more forgiving herself. She forgave her father for the unknowing ways he had hurt her. She came to realize that, as wrong as he may have been, still his intentions for her had been good, even though his behavior had hurt and frightened her as a child. She learned, over time, that in her father's youth it had been expected that a father raise his children strictly and never display weakness. Also, her dad had been treated coldly and beaten by his own father and had tried for years to convince himself that his father had intended the best for him. Even more importantly, Marian came to realize that God was not solely a demanding male warrior but could also be described like a caring and compassionate mother. Now Marian had one text from scripture that seemed always to calm her and make her realize she did not have to be afraid anymore. This is the passage: "The Lord is merciful and gracious, slow to anger and abounding in steadfast love" (Ps 103:8). Her confidence grew once her fears had subsided. And she was even able, in time, to say to her dad "I love you." She never would have dreamed it, but she couldn't help smiling and feeling warm inside when she saw the look on his face just to know that his Marian really did love him. Yes, time and her father's aging probably had contributed to the improvement in their relationship, but Marian liked to think that a loving, caring, and mothering God had a lot to do with it.

SO, THEREFORE, WHAT?

Ultimately, narratives in the Hebrew Bible that describe God as either male or female serve the purpose of demonstrating how God works through human acts, thereby preserving the ancestors of Israel in order to promote the survival and growth of the nation.[73] Although God has most often been depicted as male, the female descriptions that do exist in the text of the Hebrew Bible, when not obscured by mistranslation and misinterpretation, can shed light on a God who has what we might consider masculine power but also possesses valued aspects often seen as primarily feminine: those of affection, nurture, and protection.

In the end, we remember that we have been taught that God is a Spirit, infinitely pure and good, and that God is, of course, neither male nor female. But in searching out the only human ways that we humans have had to describe God, and in viewing aspects of God that are sometimes more masculine and other times more feminine, we can learn more about God by delving deeply into the languages of scripture and its historic backgrounds.

---

73 Bergmann, "Mothers of a Nation," 142.

CHAPTER 9

Emotions

THE QUESTION: WHICH IS GOD—JEALOUS OR ZEALOUS?

To begin, it should be noted that the words *jealous* and *zealous* have very different meanings today in the English language. *Zealous* indicates the showing of a great energy or enthusiasm in pursuit of a cause or objective.[1] The word *jealous*, on the other hand, refers to feeling or showing envy of someone over their achievements or advantages.[2] We have all observed in our lives or the lives of others around us that jealousy can be a very negative thing. It can cause anger and lead to retributive behavior. Jealousy can divide families and create rifts among friends. We all strive not to behave in jealous ways. So what does it mean when the biblical text uses the same word for both *zealous* and *jealous*?

LOOKING AT THE TEXTS

In a biblical context, there are translations in which God is said to be either jealous or zealous. In the LB the passage Exodus 20:5

1 *OED*, "zealous," accessed March 2, 2025, www.oed.com?dictionary/zealous_adj?tab=factsheet#13667475.

2 *OED*, "jealous," accessed March 2, 2025, www.oed.com/dictionary/jealous_adj?tab=factsheet#40335539.

is paraphrased as "I the Lord your God am very possessive. I will not share your affection with any other god" (LB). The GW says, "I the Lord your God am a God who does not tolerate rivals." The old WYC puts it this way: "I am thy Lord God, a strongly jealous lover." The problem is directly related in these cases to the decisions of the translators. The Hebrew word קִנְאָה (*qinah*)[3] primarily indicates a strong emotion of jealousy or zeal. It can refer to either a positive or a negative form of jealousy. In a positive sense, it describes God's zealous protection of the people and God's desire for their exclusive devotion. So in a biblical context, God's jealousy can be described as zeal, a protective kind of love that motivates God against whatever or whoever may threaten God's relationship with God's people. But when we see the word translated as "jealous" or "jealousy," this word tends to arouse in us the negative aspect of the emotion. It is clear, as we come to separate these two very different meanings of the word, that the translation here is of vital importance.

Below are some further examples of the different translations. In Exodus 20:5, the meaning seems to be "jealous," as the passage says, "You shall not bow down to them [idols] or serve them, for I the Lord your God am a jealous God." This is repeated at Exodus 34:14. Deuteronomy 4:24 also says, "a jealous God." Nahum 1:2 describes God as "jealous and avenging." At Ezekiel 39:25 (ESV), God says, "I will be jealous for my holy name." Psalm 78:58 says, "They moved him to jealousy with their idols." Zechariah 1:14 says, "Thus says the Lord of Hosts: I am very zealous for Jerusalem and for Zion."

At Isaiah 37:31–32, however, the word is positive, speaking of God returning the remnant, so the translation is most often offered as "zeal" of the Lord. The EASY even calls the word "great love." In this case, that seems appropriate. The ESV says, "The zeal of the Lord will do this." Variations from the word *zeal* or *jealousy* exist in various translations. These include: "The Lord all powerful will do this" (ESV), "great love" (EASY and NIRV), "The Lord is determined

3 BDB 888b.

to do this" (GNT), "The Lord is eager to cause this to happen" (LB), "intense passion" (VOICE), and "fervent love" (WYC).

SCENARIO

Pedro, as long as he could remember, had always realized he was a jealous person. He had wondered sometimes if jealousy might just be a part of his nature. Whenever someone he knew had better things or a better life than he did, he would feel strongly jealous of them and feelings of anger would well up in him. "Why don't I have a chance to take that trip like my friend Alfred did?" he'd ask himself. "Why does Leo seem to have such better clothes than I do?" "Why does Carlo have a girlfriend, and why can't I find one?" "How is it that Isabella is getting to go to Harvard when I can only afford to attend state college?" This behavior went on well into his late twenties. Pedro believed deep down that he could not change in this regard. He did not like this about himself but would say in his heart, "I guess it's just a part of who I am." He did realize, of course, that a lot of not-so-positive things were also happening to the people he knew. Pedro was greatly relieved it had not happened to him when his cousin Marty came down with cancer and suffered so much. He recognized too that he must be very blessed not to have been in the car with his three pals who got into a terrible car crash last Christmas. Right now, he was feeling particularly jealous because his friend Adrian had found a wonderful partner. Olivia was beautiful and intelligent, and the two of them seemed also to really enjoy a good time. She and Adrian laughed a lot, and Pedro could see they loved each other's company. "What about me?" Pedro thought. "Will I ever find a good female companion, a wife, somebody I can really love?" And jealousy would rise inside him.

One evening, Pedro attended a Bible study group with his brother Andres. (Andres had always been very zealous about his faith, much more so than Pedro.) That night, the leader was speaking about God being "a jealous God" and, at this possibility, Pedro perked up his ears. "What?" he thought. "Surely God cannot be jealous like I am!" But as the leader continued to explain, Pedro began to realize that God was not jealous in the way that a human might be described. God was what you would call *zealous*, and this seemed to mean something quite different. To be zealous meant a person experienced energy and enthusiasm and was someone who really cared. These zealous feelings seemed to be just as strong as jealousy but were positive. After all, God was zealous! Pedro kept on thinking hard about this issue over the coming days. Would it be possible for him to eliminate his jealousy and turn his feelings into zeal for whatever the need might be? Instead of being jealous about a friend taking a trip, could Pedro maybe channel that jealousy into feeling happy for the friend or even arrange for a trip of his own? Instead of being jealous of another person's better clothes, could Pedro take that same energy and turn it into thoughts about what kind of clothes he might like to own and wear, figuring out how to pay for new clothes, or even visiting a good thrift store and choosing whatever clothes appealed to him? As for college, Pedro admitted to himself that the school he was attending was just fine for him at this time. But his attitude needed changing! He should change his jealousy to zeal and try being happy for his friend who was attending Harvard.

And as for being jealous of his friend who found a girlfriend, Pedro knew in his heart that being jealous was not an attribute. Jealousy was going to do him no good whatsoever. No. Pedro definitely needed to try to turn his jealousy into zeal! Yes, all that negative jealousy had just been wasted the entire time he was engaging in it. It had not changed anything for the better and had only made him feel worse. Pedro may have been fortunate that his jealousy had gone unnoticed by others, but it had surely had a bad effect on him. "If God has zeal," thought Pedro, "now so can I!" And Pedro pushed himself into a new phase of his life. Once he made this change, he became more attractive to others. And his new positive attitude became as evident as his new clothes. His life changed. It made a dramatic turnaround. The question for Pedro was no longer, "Can I get a girlfriend?" It was "Which one should I choose?"

SO, THEREFORE, WHAT?

God is zealous for us. If our Bible translation uses the word *zealous*, then we know this means that God truly cares about us and is not ever willing to let us go. This is good news! If the translation says, rather, that God is "jealous" on our behalf, it means the same in many ways. God does not want us giving our allegiance to other gods. (In today's world, this might include our seeking after excessive financial wealth, more beauty, more success, or fame.) Anything that leads us away from our love and fidelity to our God can cause God to be jealous/zealous.

It seems very clear, particularly in the example of the jealousy or zealousness of God, that we need not only make ourselves aware of the wide variety of translations that have been found acceptable in the biblical text but also remember that the deeper meanings of words vary and change in different languages and over time. We will note as well that every language into which the Bible is translated contains words that have deeper meanings that need to be discerned. (Thinking about this certainly brings us to a beginning of understanding the meaning of and the need for the Bible's "Tower of Babel" story!) In addition, we may also be asking ourselves whether modern people can ever truly grasp the meanings of ancient words from ancient civilizations. Yet, interestingly and thankfully, the core of the biblical message has been and continues to be handed down to us through the ages and even with the many translations.

CHAPTER 10

Work/Worship

THE QUESTION: WHAT IF GOD SEES WORK, WORSHIP, AND SERVICE AS THE SAME LIFE-GIVING ACTIVITY?

What if our work was never intended to be slave-like hard labor but rather a joyful opportunity: a gift from God that was intended to give meaning to our lives and to allow us as humans to participate in making a better world? Every kind of work, of course, is not one that makes a dynamic contribution. Still, in the larger scheme of things, the many jobs fit in as part of a bigger picture to bringing comfort to others and to making our communities better and stronger. It seems very clear when looking at the history of work in almost all cultures that this word—*work*—most often indicates a struggling kind of labor too often engaged in only to appease the greed of those in control. Aspects of work as being an opportunity for joyful service have either been lost or never existed.

LOOKING AT THE TEXTS

This volume has demonstrated so far how choices of translation can strongly affect the way a passage is perceived. But the understandings of the meaning of the same word also can vary greatly from one community or one culture to another and over time. There are situations in which the meaning of a word can change as the word shifts from language to language, sometimes more than one time. Even a slight change in meaning can, in the end, affect people's thinking, behavior, and activity. The word *work* will serve as an example.

There are several words in Biblical Hebrew that can be translated into "work" in our Bible. These include עֲבוֹדָה (*ʿăḇōḏāh*),[1] but what is often missed is that this word can mean both "work" and "worship" as well as "to serve." As such, the word implies that work was part of God's plan for humankind. Christian denominations disagree theologically on whether humans become in any way "cocreators" with God by the work that we do. Either way, if the work is right, we humans are afforded, through our work, the opportunity to participate in making a better world by the work we do. The Jewish ethical teachings book *Pirkei Avot* teaches that "the world stands on three things: Torah [study of the biblical texts], Avodah—work [which also means service and worship], and G'milut Chasidim—גְּמִילוּת חֲסָדִים [which means deep lovingkindness]."[2]

The ideal of human work is self-realization. Marx goes so far as to suggest that human beings create themselves through the work they do.[3] Work before the Fall, according to LaCocque, was "a divine gift, a way for humanity to participate in the continuing work of creation and to become human," while "through the Fall, it became toil and drudgery, destructive and negative."[4] But the recovery of work can be a redemptive and creative act, even a form of worship, art being its finest expression.[5]

---

1 BDB 712a.

2 Yosef Marcus, comp., *Pirkei Avot: Ethics of the Fathers* (Brooklyn: Kehot Publication Society, 2009).

3 Bo-Myung Seo, "The Dialectic of Praxis and the Theology of Work," in *Furthering Interfaith Biblical Scholarship: A Festschrift in Memory of André LaCocque*, ed. Doreen M. McFarlane (Eugene, OR: Pickwick, 2024), 98.

4 André LaCocque, *Work and Creativity: A Philosophical Study from Creation to Post-Modernity* (New York: Lexington, 2020), 40.

5 LaCocque, *Work and Creativity*, 40.

As mentioned earlier, over the millennia, the concept of what work is has taken many turns, and it has moved from being seen as a privilege humans are given to participate in with God to, too often, hard labor without purpose except to make the wealthy wealthier. We know only too well that work is not always satisfying and that too many people have had to work too hard. Slavery is forced work without joy. Creative serving and worshipful work are the very lifeblood of the Hebrew Bible, "flowing throughout its manifold stories, laws, and prayers. Yet, in practice—in history and in religions—this uplifting notion of work has all too easily succumbed to a very different idea and reality: drudgery, toil, onerous labor." Yeshaya Gruber asks how this could have happened and most interestingly suggests, as we are saying throughout this book, that, as usual, translation may lie at the core of this dilemma![6]

Gruber demonstrates the problem by commenting on the mutations on the meaning of *work* from the Hebrew word מְלָאכָה (*melakah*), meaning "something done," into the Greek word ἔργον (*ergon*), meaning "*work*," "*deed*," "*action*," "*task*," *or* "*labor*," and then into Slavic/Muscovite languages and religious communities and their attitudes about work. The Hebrew word *avodah* can mean "servitude" as well as "just work." It can also be rendered in Greek as *leitourgía*, meaning "*work" or "public service*." Already the person reading the Hebrew Bible / Old Testament in Greek would not be getting an absolutely accurate translation of the Hebrew word's intention. By the time the words for work were translated from the Septuagint Greek into the Slavic languages, however, work had come to be viewed as something more like liturgy than labor. Concepts had again been reshuffled. The Slavic word for work is *troud*. And this word, *troud*, is not employed even once in the East Slavic translation.[7] Various words are used for *work*, but these are "extreme modifications introduced largely by the

6 Yeshaya Gruber, "Creative and Destructive Work: Greek and Slavic Distributaries of Hebrew and Biblical Lifeblood," in McFarlane, *Furthering Interfaith Biblical Scholarship*, 109.

7 Gruber, "Creative and Destructive Work," 124.

mediation of the LXX."[8] Work, in the Slavonic monastic tradition, is seen as voluntary heavy labor, and it is viewed as a holy activity, but it means suffering for the sake of God for the purpose of growing closer to God.[9] As Gruber and his chapter suggest, translation is often to blame for misunderstandings about biblical concepts and understandings of the nature and behavior of God, and this is a good example.

In Genesis 2:15, work is presented as belonging to the very creation of the human being. Here it says, "The Lord God [*Yahweh Elohim*] took the man [human (*ha adam*)] and put him in the Garden of Eden to till [tend/work (*avodah*)] *it* and *keep* [שָׁמַר (*shamar*)] it."

Examples of translations are listed here:

> "The Lord God took the man and put him in the Garden of Eden to *work* it and *take care of* it" (NIV).

> "Then the Lord God took the man and put him in the garden of Eden to *tend* and *keep* it" (NKJV).

We can see in the examples above that the concept of tilling or working is very clear as meaning "labor" in the English translations. But nowhere to be found is that aspect of the work being equal to or the same as worship. If indeed the Hebrew word does include that concept, have we no word in English that could encompass its meaning? And if we had such a word that could have been chosen, might the very nature of work have evolved differently? Might the word *serve* have better served the meaning to help us understand?

Work, in Jewish tradition, is a מצוה (*mitzvah*) (*good deed*) that brings about its own reward. In Tannaitic times (approximately 10–220 CE), work and the worker were held in high esteem within Judaism and considered secondary only to the study of the Torah,

8 Gruber, "Creative and Destructive Work," 124.

9 Gruber, "Creative and Destructive Work," 125.

while in Greek thought, work was considered unworthy.[10] And, biblically speaking, no work is lower or higher than another. Work means encountering the other and the world. Labor belongs to the already / not yet of eschatology. And that "not yet" informs the principle of hope.[11]

SCENARIO

Josh could well have been described as a "man of faith." He had trusted in God all his life, studied his Bible, and been involved with his church. But Josh always had thought of himself as just a common man, an ordinary person. When Josh was younger, he could put in a twelve-hour day working with his hands. He never really made a lot of money, but he was able to support first his parents and then also a wife and four children.

The only trouble with Josh was that he let people take advantage of him—especially his bosses. When others said they had to get home, Josh would be willing to work late. When others took vacations, Josh would take up the slack. And it's not that he enjoyed his work. Work was always a burden to him. And, over time, it started to take its toll on his body. Josh was getting older, and his body was making that very clear to him with arthritis, backache, and knee problems.

After many years, Josh was not able to work at all anymore. One afternoon, his pastor came over to visit him, and Josh poured out his heart to him. "Pastor Dave, you know I worked so very hard all my life. When I look back, I think I did it all wrong. I should have spent more time on my faith. I should have been at worship. Too many times, I spent my Sundays at work." Pastor Dave responded that,

10 Joseph Heinemann, "The Status of the Labourer in Jewish Law and Society in the Tannaitic Period," *Hebrew Union College Annual* 25 (1954): 263–325, https://www.jstor.org/stable/i23502447.

11 LaCocque, *Work and Creativity*, 76. LaCocque speaks of Ernst Bloch's *The Principle of Hope*, trans. Neville Plaice and Paul Knight, 3 vols. (Cambridge, MA: MIT Press, 1986).

yes, Josh had probably worked far too hard. But he pointed out to him something that really surprised him. "You know, work can be a form of worship," Pastor Dave said. "As a matter of fact, the Hebrew word in the Old Testament, *avodah*, means 'service.' It means 'work,' but, surprisingly enough, it also means 'worship.'" Josh was truly struck by this little bit of scholarly information. Why had nobody told him this before? Why, it looked like all the work he had done so vigorously—to build a better building, or to feed his family, or to help in his community—was also all for God; in his loving service he had been worshipping all along! Josh could not contain his joy. His life had not been wasted after all. Josh had been working for God. He had been working alongside God. That felt very, very good!

SO, THEREFORE, WHAT?

Could the world have been different if they'd told us? What if our religious leaders had known the biblical languages well enough, or the translators had been more careful to explain, that the Bible also meant worship and service when it spoke about work? If the purpose of work had not deteriorated over time, or had the word's complex meaning at least not been lowered to suggest only painfully hard labor, what might our world look like now? Over the centuries, so many people have suffered with overwork and with guilt if they have not done what they consider enough work. And what about those who, over many centuries, have gained much at the expense of those who worked under their control? Over centuries, slaves were worked to death. Even paid laborers were overworked to the point of death. The Industrial Revolution brought labor to a breaking point so that, in time, at least in certain places, the workers organized themselves into unions and their demands had to be responded to. Still, in our own time, many unfair working conditions continue to exist throughout the world. We cannot help but ask if lives could have been different were it not for the incredible greed on the part of people in power.

Although many have suffered too much from the demands made by those who employ them, there are still, of course, circumstances in which we have worked but not really understood the good purposes that work can have. For any number of reasons, we have not been able to take real joy in the work we do, not realizing that it's not only silent prayer or church attendance that pleases God but also the daily labor that each of us has engaged in, working to make things better for others, for our own loved ones, and for our communities.

As for those who have abusively caused the suffering of others by forcing them to work for long hours, in poor working conditions, and in ways that increase the imbalance of justice among people, their lives too would change if their understandings about work could be changed and new understandings brought forth. Greed on the part of those who gain from it may seem advantageous for a time but can ultimately be hurtful to the perpetrators as well as to the victims.

With a clearer understanding of the translation of the word *avodah* (work) to mean not only "labor" but also "service" and "worship," we can come to view that God has lovingly and generously given us work as an opportunity to participate in the ongoing future of this world in which we live! It is never too late to "reclaim the Biblical Hebrew notion of creative serving, sometimes sacrificial work (physical, mental, and spiritual)"[12] as our joyful purpose in this world.

---

12 Gruber, "Creative and Destructive Work," 126.

CHAPTER 11

Names of God

THE QUESTIONS: WHY MIGHT GOD HAVE BEEN GIVEN SO MANY DIFFERENT NAMES OVER HISTORY? DOES USING A PARTICULAR NAME FOR GOD CHANGE OUR WAYS OF RELATING TO GOD AND EACH OTHER?

As we move toward the conclusion of this volume, it is valuable to examine the variety of names that have been given to God in the Bible and consider how some of these have been translated—and how, at times, the mistranslating of them may have affected our feelings about our relationship with God. Can we even know God's name? Does God have a name? Are we permitted to know and speak God's name?

Perhaps it is best to begin by listing some of the names of God as found in our Bible. There are many. Some are more ancient and currently out of use, but it is good to recall these names in their contexts.

LOOKING AT THE TEXTS

God. In English, of course, we have the name God, the word that most of us employ. It is a generic word in the Bible and in our spoken language that, when capitalized, represents the God we worship. The

English word God derives from the Proto-Germanic word *guðan*. It was likely based on the root of a word that meant "to call" or "to invoke." We use the word *god* when we speak of gods other than our God. The name of Yahweh or YHWH will be discussed further on in this section.

Elohim is a name used for God in the Hebrew Bible, although the word is actually plural. The letters *im* at the end of a word indicate the plural, although Elohim is not intended to be plural when used as a name of God. This plural word is also employed to name the gods of Egypt at Exodus 12:12. When speaking about our God, the plural is used, which may be to indicate honor. (For example, British royalty occasionally uses plural references, such as the monarch saying something like "We are not amused!" This is commonly known as "the royal *we*.")

YHWH Elohim is used for God. YHWH, or Yahweh, also known as the Tetragrammaton (meaning "four letters"), is virtually untranslatable but said traditionally to mean something like "I am what I am." (Elohim, earlier, had represented the primary God of a pantheon of gods.) Here, the name is an acceptable Hebrew construct of two nouns, so would simply be translated into English as "God" or "the Lord God."

Adonai is a word often used for God. It means, in Hebrew, "master," "Lord," or "my Lord."

El Shaddai, as discussed in detail in chapter eight, has a complex and controversial meaning that may be male or possibly female. This biblical term for God comes from very ancient sources. As such, its true meaning cannot be discerned. Strangely, it is almost always translated as "God Almighty," but this has no known etymology. A more ancient meaning could possibly even be "God with breasts."[1] This could suggest that perceptions of God in ancient times emanated from agricultural communities with fertility concerns. When the

1 Doreen M. McFarlane, "Lost in Translation: The Sexuality of God in Scripture," in *Scriptural Sexualities*, ed. Zohar Hadromi-Allouche, Nirmal Fernando, and Keren Abbou Hershkovitz. Publication forthcoming.

term is employed in Isaiah, Joel, and Job, it implies power and might. Yet in Genesis it seems to be more deeply connected in some way to fertility. Nevertheless, we do know that Exodus 6:2 says, "God also spoke to Moses and said to him. I am the Lord [YHWH]. I appeared to Abraham, Isaac, and Jacob as God Almighty (El Shaddai), but by name 'The Lord' [YHWH] I did not make myself known to them."

El Roi is the name of God spoken by Hagar in Genesis 16:13. It has been translated as "God who sees me" or "God of sight."

El Elyon occurs twenty-eight times in the Hebrew Bible and is translated as "Most High God." It appears first in Genesis 14:18 and appears nineteen times in the Psalms.

Yahweh Jireh means "Yahweh will provide" and appears at Genesis 22:14 at the binding of Isaac.

Yahweh Raah means "Yahweh is [my] shepherd" (Ps 23:1).

Yahweh Nissi means "The Lord is my banner" (Exod 17:15).

Ish means "husband" (man). At Hosea 2:16 and 2:19–20, God is described metaphorically as a husband, saying "on that day, says the Lord, you will call me 'my husband' . . . I will take you for my wife forever; I will take you for my wife in righteousness and in justice, in steadfast love and in mercy, I will take you for my wife in faithfulness, and you shall know the Lord." Aside from describing the love and loyalty God pronounces to creation, this text offers people who choose to be in the bonds of human relationship a role model of love and loyalty!

Ha Shem literally means "The Name" in Hebrew. This name is often engaged in conversation about God because, in Judaism, it is inappropriate to speak aloud the name of God. In prayer, the name Adonai is often employed, but when not in prayer, Ha Shem is. This word for God appears in the Bible at Leviticus 24:11 and Deuteronomy 28:58.

There are various additional names for God in the Hebrew Bible, but those listed above are the main ones. And, of course, Christianity gives God the name of Trinity—indicating the triune nature of God as Father, Son, and Holy Spirit; three in one; or Creator, Redeemer, and Sanctifier. The issue of mistranslations from the Greek in the

New Testament is complex and shall have to be reserved for a future volume. But, of course, God is also known as Abba (Daddy), as well as the Rock and "the Alpha and Omega" (the beginning and the end), along with other beloved monikers.

These many names for God can tell us much about the nature of God. And the names employed have varied over time. Naming God as a shepherd goes back at least as far as the communities at Ugarit. The cuneiform tablets of Ugarit naming God as shepherd derive from 1300–1200 BCE. Of course, in a sheepherding culture it seems likely God would have been seen this way, as one who watches over and cares for the people as a shepherd does for the flock. God's names as provider and strength and rock are also about protecting and caring for the people. As discussed earlier, the term El Shaddai may possibly have an earlier meaning related to breasts and nurturing in times when fertility was a major issue and later took on a meaning of warlike power and strong protection when the people of Israel were in trouble with other nations. El Elyon, as mentioned above, indicates the greatest respect, pointing out that our God is the highest of the pantheon of gods as believed in during ancient times and that are mentioned in various parts of the Bible. God moves in history from being the head god of this pantheon to being the one and only God. God is also known as Ha Shem, when people were not to speak God's name aloud, because Ha Shem means "The Name."

It cannot be denied that the God of the Hebrew Bible does make demands and threats at times and expects unequivocal loyalty. We also read in places that God, sometimes on our behalf, is willing to slay and does slay thousands. We must keep in mind, however, that such narratives were offered to indicate that, whatever happened, our God remained in charge and all-powerful. Even when bad things happened, the writers of the Bible did not want to give credit to anyone but God, as that would indicate that God was not in full power. They even often blamed themselves for things that have gone wrong to keep God's name intact.

YHWH (or Yahweh) is the name (or non-name) that the Bible tells us God gives God's self at Exodus 3:14. The Hebrew word is virtually nontranslatable although it has been historically described as meaning something like "I am what I am." The Hebrew word is something like "to be" but implying past, present, and future, suggesting immutability. In ancient times, to know and speak someone's name was believed to give one power over them. And, of course, no human could have any power over God. It is forbidden for Jewish people to speak aloud this holy name, and, for this reason, alternate names have been used such as Elohim or Adonai. The earliest known reference for God as Yahweh is found on the Mesha Stele, which dates to 840 BCE.[2]

It was believed for centuries that the above name (Yahweh or YHWH) was **Jehovah**. Strangely, this name came into existence by way of a misunderstanding. Some Christian in the sixteenth century, possibly a friar named Galatinus, seems to have created this name, Jehovah, by placing together the consonants of Yahweh with the vowels of Adonai, apparently having seen it written that way. He did not realize that the Jewish people were writing it this way to avoid speaking the holy name aloud. This error continued among Christians and the name Jehovah for them became a most beloved and powerful title for God.[3]

The name of YHWH or Yahweh in its essence seems to at least include a sense of the hiddenness of God. Much theology has been written over the centuries regarding the hiddenness of God, often referring to God as *deus absconditus*, meaning "hidden" or "concealed." Throughout the Bible, writers have referred to God as being hidden. An example is Isaiah 45:15, which says: "Truly, you are a God who hides himself, O God of Israel, the Savior." At Job 13:24, Job asks God: "Why do you hide your face and count me your enemy?" Micah 3:4 speaks of leaders who do harm to the people of God. It is

---

2 The Mesha Stele, also known as the Moabite Stone, of around 840 BCE, contains this Canaanite inscription. It is currently housed at the Louvre in Paris.

3 It has been used almost up until today and is still present in English texts of oratorios and classical songs. (For example, the English translation of Franz Schubert's song "Die Allmacht" begins with the words "Great Is Jehovah the Lord.")

said here that "then they will cry to the Lord, but he will not answer them; he will hide his face from them at that time because they have acted wickedly." But God is not always hidden because the people have sinned. Most of us have probably experienced personally a sense of the hiddenness of God. "I am what I am" at the very least suggests that God's name is purely God's business. This name strongly hints at the fact that we cannot really know or entirely understand God or discern God's motives.

The name YHWH seems to also imply an unspoken "and it's not your business." God has a privacy that we cannot discern and need not even try to do so. This brings us to the vital point that God is totally "other"; God is different from everyone and everything else.

SCENARIO

Melissa had been raised without being part of a specific faith community. It had seemed perfectly logical to her parents around the time she was a small child to keep religion out of her life. The reason they had was that they came from two very different religions and cultures. (Her dad was a Hindu and had immigrated from India when he was a young doctor. Her mother had been a practicing Roman Catholic. Melissa's mother's grandfather was Catholic as far back as his roots could take him, and her grandmother had grown up as a Methodist but raised Melissa's mother as a Catholic to follow the expectations of her husband's church.) So Melissa's parents had made the decision to simply raise her to be a good person and, after she'd reached age eighteen, let her decide for herself which religious community she would join.

Unfortunately, the problem was that Melissa was raised with no background from which to choose a faith. She had never attended services. She'd never been to Sunday school with other children. Her parents had made a special effort not to discuss religion or argue about religious concepts at home. Whenever anything remotely close to a religious issue came up, they would intentionally grow silent when in her presence! Melissa had been allowed to attend one or two rallies and church-type events with friends over the years. But she had never been in any religion-connected club or group of people her age. By the time she went to school, anything related in any way to religion had been removed from the public school system. No Bible readings, no Lord's Prayer recitation, and not even the singing of any Christmas carols. So Melissa had been raised without any faith base from which to choose. In the place of religion, she had been taught by her parents over the years about helping others, behaving kindly to everyone, and engaging regularly in volunteerism—all good things.

The only problem with what seemed like her parents' flawless plan was that Melissa had always had strong spiritual feelings. It just seemed to be part of her nature. She secretly felt jealous of her friends when they spoke about their religious communities. It seemed inappropriate for her to bring up the subject with her parents. Besides, she simply did not have the vocabulary for it. She couldn't ask them for advice or have any kind of discussion or argument with them about religion because she would not have even known where to begin. Melissa kept telling herself that she didn't really want any faith or church or religious life. But, deep inside, she could never convince herself. She just didn't know and could not articulate what it was she wanted. It felt like a longing, an unspoken emptiness.

It was the last place anyone could have guessed that Melissa would find God—the public library! Yes, it truly was that place. Without having to feel embarrassed, at the age of seventeen, Melissa simply walked up to the local librarian who was sitting at the front desk and asked her this question. She said, "I was wondering if you could recommend a book or books that teach about world religions, and maybe another one that tells about the religious communities a person might find here, in this city." Well, it is a fact that there is nothing a librarian loves more than being asked for books they recommend. "Someone wants to learn something," the librarian thought, "and that person is asking me to do the very thing I was trained for—they're asking what books they should read and where to find them!" The librarian happily went to work and prepared for Melissa a list of books and journals that were available right there for her to borrow that day. And she assured her there were many more. She could get as deeply into this as she chose! Melissa read the books voraciously and then went back for more. She was feeling somehow as if she'd been starved for this information. She was amazed. She was fascinated. With some of the religious ideas she read she was surprised, and with others she was a bit shocked. Who could have ever expected religion to be so diverse and so exciting? Eventually, Melisssa settled down to reading more about one Christian denomination that appealed to her. She decided, after a few months, that she would call a local pastor, as there was a church not far from her of that denomination. Pastors, much like librarians, seem really pleased to have the opportunity to speak about their church and beliefs. In time, Melissa started attending that church. (Her parents seemed OK with it.) Eventually, she became a member and got quite involved in service with that community.

As Melissa thought about how she had come to faith in her own way and in her own time, she recalled that one main reason she had not been able to believe in God was that it seemed no one had been able to explain to her who God was! In the end, strangely, no one and even no book had been able to explain God. The more Melissa read about God or talked about God, the more confused she had become. In the end, when she decided to become a Christian and a part of this Christian community, she had come to realize that God is and always will be a mystery. But she had also come to know that God can only really be known through God's incredible acts of love and forgiveness and of hope and support that we know God has displayed since the first words of the Bible were written. The names of God that Melissa had learned through her reading—the names of YHWH, and Elohim, and Adonai, and El Shaddai, and Rock, and Shepherd, and, for her as a Christian, Trinity (Father, Son, and Holy Spirit)—all to Melissa meant one thing: they meant that she was loved by her Creator and that we all are loved. God is with us. We are not alone! Melissa now understood that she not only was a child of God now, but all through the time she'd been searching, and the time she had not even known she was searching, she had already been a beloved child of this mysterious God who loves her more than she could ever know.

She realized too that her parents were loved by God and that they were not to blame for holding her back. They had never intended to do that. They had only seen themselves as affording her the opportunity to find all this marvelous good news for herself. Yes, God loved them too and had always loved them.

SO, THEREFORE, WHAT?

It seems unlikely that we humans will ever really be able to get a sure grasp on either the name of God or the complete identity of God for humankind. Our God is simply too big for us to fathom! At the same time, this same God has found manifold ways over time, and still today—in actions and in words (through scripture)—to prove to us that we are found to be valuable to God. And perhaps it is because we can never fully know God that we have chosen to give God so many names.

It is interesting to note which name various individuals choose to use for God and in prayer. Jewish people might address God as Ha Shem ("The Name") or as Adonai (which means "My Lord"). God is also called Elokeinu Melekhaolam, which means "Our God, King of the Universe." Conservative Christians often address God in prayer as Father God. More generally liberal Christians might say Dear God, Gracious God, or Creator God (the latter at least partly in order not to use sexist language). Many Christians choose to pray directly to Jesus, addressing him also as Savior, brother, or as God's beloved son. Some Pentecostal groups will pray directly to the Holy Spirit.

CHAPTER 12

Creation

THE QUESTION: WHAT IS THIS THING CALLED "CREATING" THAT GOD DOES, AND DO WE HUMANS ALSO CREATE?

Yes, as expressed above in the variety of names of God, and in the fact that the main name, Yahweh, although virtually untranslatable may suggest something like "I am what I am," God is still in many ways unknowable. Although humans can relate to and be in relationship with God throughout the Hebrew Bible / Old Testament, it is still vitally important that we maintain our humility and always remember the place of humans in the scheme of things. This fact is driven home in powerful ways in Job and, importantly, by one single Hebrew word that is somewhat misunderstood in translation by those of us who speak English. That word is *bara*, translated into English as "create." There is nothing wrong with using this word, as that is exactly what it means! The problems begin when we come to learn that this Hebrew verb בָּרָא (*bara*) is something that can only be done by God. No human can do *bara*. We see this word in the Bible at Genesis, of course, where God is creating the heavens and the earth and everything else. So all the things that humans do for which we employ the English word *create* are entirely different from the creating that God does in Hebrew scripture. Hebrew has the word *bara* for what God does, and other words— לַעֲשׂוֹת (*la-asot*) (make, labor, work, act), להכין (*le-hakyn*) (prepare, make ready, get ready), and ליצור (*li-tzor*) (make, form, manufacture, mold, generate)—for the kind of so-called creating that humans do.

LOOKING AT THE TEXTS

To begin, of course, we have the creation narratives. The first words of the Bible are the words בְּרֵאשִׁית בָּרָא אֱלֹהִים אֵת הַשָּׁמַיִם וְאֵת הָאָרֶץ (*barashit bara Elohim et shamaim v-et ha aretz*)—"In the beginning [or "about beginnings"] God created the heaven [sky] and the earth [ground]" (Gen 1:1) (KJV). As mentioned above, this verb בָּרָא (*bara*) represents the work of creating that only God, and no human, can do. Throughout the Bible, this word, *bara*, continues to be something only God can do. Here are a few examples: Genesis 1:21, 27; 2:3; 5:1, 2; 6:7; Deuteronomy 4:32, Psalms 51:10; 89:12; Isaiah 4:5; 40:26; Jeremiah 31:22; Amos 4:13; and Malachi 2:10.

In English, the word is used differently, for what God and also for what humans do. The *OED* describes the word *create* as "of a divine being or natural agency; to bring into being or cause to exist; to produce where nothing was before."[1] Merriam-Webster, however, adds "to invest with a new form or office [e.g., 'She was created a lieutenant'], or "to produce or bring about a course of action or behavior [e.g., 'her arrival created a fuss'.]" Importantly, it can also mean "to produce through imaginative skill [e.g., 'to create a painting,']" or to design, as in, for example, "She creates dresses."[2] But, in English, this word *create* would also be used for what God has done. Although most Bible translators into English have chosen other words to describe the "creative" work that humans do, English-speaking Bible readers still do not generally recognize and acknowledge the uniqueness of the Hebrew word *bara* that is

1 *OED*, "create," accessed March 11, 2025, https://www.oed.com/dictionary/create_v?tab=factsheet#8012857.

2 *Merriam-Webster Collegiate Dictionary*, 10th ed. (1999), s.v. "create."

translated into "create" when they read only their English versions. The reason, of course, is that it has a more casual meaning in so many circumstances in our English language.

This unique work of God is brought to light in a profound way in the book of Job. As discussed in chapter three, Job, who has been a wealthy and successful man, has lost everything, including his health and physical comfort, and he complains bitterly to God, calling God forth and demanding to speak to God face to face. Job's friends try everything in their power to get Job to back off and apologize, but Job stands his ground. When God at last comes forward, finally speaking to Job, God seems to bully Job all the way through from chapter 38 to 41. God powerfully and repeatedly reminds Job that only God is creator of everything. The powerful words of this text are so magnificent and overwhelming that one could feel almost as if God has composed them.[3] We know of course that they must have been composed by humans, but we can sense in these verses the powerful inspirer that brought them to the human mind.

Here are just a few examples.

> Job 38:4–5: "Where were you when I laid the foundations of the earth? Tell me, if you have understanding. Who determined its measurements—surely you know!"
>
> Job 39:1–2: "Do you know when the mountain goats give birth? Do you observe the calving of the deer? Can you number the months that they fulfil? And do you know the time they give birth?"

The passage goes on with God speaking. God asks Job if he (and humans) can get the wild ox to serve them, if he understands the behavior of the wild ostrich, if he gave the horse its strength, or if it is by his wisdom that the hawk soars.

---

3 In the 1980s, pastor and biblical scholar Walter Brueggeman spoke of this, with great conviction, at an evangelism conference in Chicago before a large audience.

If we would take the time to read and really digest the incredible words of God in Job 38–41, we might begin to understand the power of that one little Hebrew word *bara*. This word means "to create" but only and always refers to the doings of God and no one else.

One vital volume to consult when studying the Bible, and especially in this instance, is what is known as the Septuagint, referred to in print as LXX. The Septuagint is the Hebrew Bible / Old Testament translated from Hebrew into Greek. Scholars generally agree that this translating took place from the third century to the first century BCE. The Septuagint is important to biblical scholarship because it was translated at a much earlier time, so the translation reflects to some degree mindsets and cultures that were closer to those at the time of the Hebrew text. By examining the Septuagint Greek, we can observe that the Greek also lacks a separate, specific word for "to create" that coincides with the Hebrew word *bara*. So, in the Septuagint, Genesis 1:1 says, ἐν ἀρχῇ ἐποίησεν ὁ θεὸς (*en archen epoinsen o theos*). In this passage, and those that follow that speak of what God does but also of what humans do, the verbs to describe what we do are shared between what God does and what we do. Of the religious books, only in the Hebrew is that one word of creation reserved only for God.

So, it seems clear that to learn and understand the word *bara* that was employed in the original language in the Hebrew Bible to describe something that only God does is to learn much about our Creator that we simply could not have known from only an English translation.

SCENARIO

Sam would never have admitted it to anyone else, but secretly he had always wanted to be famous. He didn't care much about money, really. He did not seem to need what so many of his friends went after. They longed to live in a beautiful home. Or they wanted a big boat with an even bigger motor that could speed them across to the other side of the lake. They wanted to have fun too. They spoke and daydreamed about parties with lots of magnificent food and drink. Some of his friends and family had higher ideals and hoped to find the perfect partner, the best lover, or a good-looking and well-heeled spouse so they could have babies without worrying about finances. All their dreams were fine, but, secretly of course, Sam just wanted to be highly respected and famous.

It took him a few years before he even came to a decision about what kind of fame he wanted to have. He tried out music as a teen but learned quickly that he was greatly lacking in that department. He considered sports but, alas, the sporting world had little interest in him. He did a little car racing but found it just too dangerous.

Eventually, Sam settled in on wanting to be a painter, an artist. He set out and took several courses, first online and then in person. He started painting just for himself. He understood, as his art teachers had explained, that, like a singer, he'd first have to "find his voice." He discovered that what he loved the most were landscapes, so he started dreaming about becoming known for painting these. He had a pretty good office job but, in time, learned that to be good at one's art, one had to work at it full-time. He quit his day job and got part-time work in a coffee shop so he'd have more time to paint. He would go out into the country and to the nearby seaside to paint as often as he could.

The problem, he soon came to realize, turned out to be that God was a much more accomplished artist than he. He learned it one day at sunset when he was sitting out on the beach. He'd seen scenery of sunsets before, but this one, like all the others, simply could not be captured. Sam mixed the colors on his palette, but they could not touch the glory of the colors he was observing across the sky before him. He tried to paint the setting sun as it descended below the horizon, but God had made it perfect, as God did every night without any painter.

At first, when Sam realized what it meant, Sam began to weep (and he was normally no weeper). "God is bigger" were the words that kept filling his heavy heart. "God is the artist." At this point,

Sam was able to admit to himself something more as well. He realized that God gives each of us gifts with which to give him glory. Some are musicians and some are painters and some live what might be ordinary lives. But everyone is valuable. Yes, even Sam. He did not have to become famous to be valuable in this world. We are all of value. He realized at that moment that God had not chosen to make him a great artist or maybe a great anything. And that was all right.

Sam stayed at that beach until the sun descended and all was in darkness. And then, in the darkness, he simply picked up his things and walked out into his future. He didn't know anything about what that future would bring, but he sensed that it would be good. After all, God had spread before him that night the most beautiful painting that ever could be—God's own night sky.

SO, THEREFORE, WHAT?

It seems only appropriate that our response in the final chapter regarding the behavior and attributes of God that can be learned from the original language would be this one: God is bigger than we can fathom. God is greater. God is more powerful. And God is also more loving and caring than we can ever know. Importantly also, we need to realize and accept that God is always "other"—that is, qualitatively different from ourselves. God is infinite Spirit, and we never come close to being gods or even god-like. We are human, and as Genesis clearly declares, we are made from dust. In other words, God is always Creator, and we are always Created! For this reason, we are called to bow ourselves in humility before such a presence. Still, we have learned throughout the biblical text that this same God loves us, cares about us, listens to us, and forgives us. Even more importantly, God seeks always to be in relationship with us as humans. There are, as mentioned earlier, times when God appears to be hidden from us and we cannot explain this absence, but it is always temporary.

From this chapter, we must also learn a different kind of humility. And that is that, however educated we may become, we can only see the truth from our small perspective—that is, from the lens of the language (or languages) that we speak and the culture and timeframe in which we live. God is always bigger than all of this, and that is good news.

CHAPTER 13

The Good News

In the end, it is impossible to accurately describe God. After all, all we have are our own human words and human thoughts to describe a God who is beyond description. We have learned throughout the course of this volume that looking at a variety of alternate biblical translations at times can show the "good news" of the Bible to be even better than we had anticipated. Insights into the meaning of the texts can continue to be unearthed when we take the time to explore the biblical texts and languages in their contexts. Here, we have learned and examined further many aspects of God that are present in scripture. These include a variety of matters regarding the nature and behavior of God. The God of the Bible has perhaps appeared at first to be hierarchical, but we have learned how God created male and female to be equal companions in this world. Then, we discovered that it might be very possible and even acceptable for us to argue with God without God's becoming angry or seeking to punish us. God, in fact, may even desire to reward us for our honesty in the relationship. We've learned that when humans convince God that, in their view, God has done something wrong, God can be ready and willing to listen and even say "I am sorry" and cease any harm to us that God may have considered. We find out also that God may not have the same idea of who the enemies are as we do. Our sworn enemies may at times, in fact, not be God's enemies at all. We have learned about the nature of God's unending and incredible love for us as well as God's steadfast loyalty and willingness to help us, no matter how weak we may be or become.

We have learned that, even though our essence as humans may consist of various parts, including body, soul, and spirit, God still sees us as undivided and as whole beings, and it can be good for our emotional health for us to see ourselves this way as well. We have learned too that the resurrection of the dead has been promised to us, but that the afterlife is likely always to remain a mystery and in the hands of our maker if we are still living on this earth. Still, we can be assured we are always safe with God during and after our human life. We have studied and learned much about God in relation to sexuality. God has been described throughout the Bible in terms that are both male and female because God surely embraces the attributes of both, as we know them. God has been perceived at times in history as male and at other times as having female attributes. Yet God is, of course, not either one but rather is pure spirit. Next, we have considered what was meant by *work* in the attitudes and behavior taught to us in the Hebrew Bible. We seem to have lost, through translation, the joyful enterprise that God intended our work/labor to be. We have learned that work, according to the Hebrew text, can embrace labor, liturgy/worship, and service! The work that we do was intended to be our purpose for living and something that brings us joy and fulfillment. We have considered the many names of God and what they can mean for our understanding of our Creator. And, finally, we have had a look at the kind of creating that God does in comparison to what we do in this world. But, still, in the end it seems our God is indescribable in human terms. In the Biblical Hebrew original, we have learned that God is the only real Creator, although we humans do have the opportunity to participate in the future. We have the work of moving things around!

ABOUT THE TRANSLATIONS YOU CHOOSE

In most cases, creating good translations of the Bible seems to require, at the very least, groups or committees familiar with the biblical languages. The members of such a group should not be of only one gender or one age group, and ideally they ought to come from a variety of cultures and traditions. Even with such a group carefully gathered, history continues to show that it is never easy to come up with excellent translations. People with the best intentions have disagreed more than agreed and too often had to compromise. The ways we translate and employ language in our own times and coming from our own cultural experiences will often greatly affect how we perceive and then translate biblical texts. How can we then ever arrive at good translations, and how can we know how accurate they might be?[1]

Robert Alter, a scholar who possesses intimate knowledge of the Hebrew Bible and who has produced his own personal translation of the entire Bible, points out that even well-intentioned committees are not always the best at choosing the most appropriate words and phrases to employ in a biblical translation. The reason is that, even after much deliberation, a committee's agreed-upon meaning may be one that is politically correct and that will keep the peace within the committee.[2] But that does not necessarily make it the most accurate translation. Just as an example, such translations often miss important nuances related to the rhythm and flow of the language that only a native speaker would recognize and appreciate. After all, the Bible was not written by committees!

---

1 In 1971, a paraphrased version of the Bible was written by one man, Kenneth Taylor. It became the *LB*. Although surely well intentioned, it could not be accurate because it was the paraphrased work of one man not familiar with Hebrew or Greek and who worked only from the 1901 *ASV*. In time, ninety scholars labored with the original Greek and Hebrew to create the *NLT*. One hundred scholars working directly from what they call "the best available Hebrew, Aramaic, and Greek texts," starting in 1965, produced what is now the NIV. The notes claim that this group was widely transdenominational and included many updates and revisions. As ancient languages have come to be better understood in recent decades due to new archaeological discoveries and computer technologies, translations continue to be reviewed and revised while keeping continuity with known traditions. All translators and related groups make interpretive decisions, so the results will always be less than pure.

2 Alter, *Art of Bible Translation*.

Even in the best translations, words will fall short, especially when attempts are made to describe the indescribable deity. It is not always possible to even know whether the writers of scripture of specific times intended to depict a God corporeally present or tried to describe the acts of a God who was solely spirit and wholly *other*. In either case, it seems inevitable that human-like depictions of God (including even in sexual terms) would be employed by those who wrote and interpreted scripture. It has been shown here that the Hebrew Bible generally depicts God as a male and possessing a male body. Descriptions of God possessing female body parts (e.g., breasts or womb)[3] or exhibiting feminine behavior are also clearly present but have been repressed, often by means of biased choices in translation.

When a word can be translated into English by any number of words with similar but varying meanings, it has been suggested that it could at times be useful for the translator(s) to simply place the original Hebrew word in that place and add the most accurate English translations in parentheses or even in a footnote. Further translations could then be revised as new interpretations surface relating to them. According to Yitzik Peleg, "Two readings imply two understandings, and at least two meanings . . . two meanings in a biblical text are reflected within that text itself and do not come from the imagination or wishful thinking of the reader. The reader . . . understands too that not everything is obvious and is open to more than one truth in a text."[4] Language is ambiguous, and, in Hebrew, the same word may even have opposite meanings. Peleg points out that the ambiguity or the wordplay used by the narrator creates tension and enriches the story and, by that, further enriches our delight of it as readers. What has been lost in translation, he suggests, could be reclaimed as readers look at alternate reading possibilities, and texts of the Bible can be brought to new life. This could surely prove

3 As discussed in chapter eight.

4 Yitzik Peleg. "Two Readings: Sexual Verbs and Ambiguity in the Biblical Story", in *Scriptural Sexualities*, eds. Zohar Hadromi-Allouche, Nirmal Fernando, and Keren Abbou Hershkovitz. Publication forthcoming.

useful in increasing our understanding of the biblical depictions of God. If the regular Bible reader had access to the various possible meanings of a word that person was reading, this would allow the reader the opportunity to consider the options!

IN CONCLUSION

The intention of this book has been to present the reader with a variety of alternate ideas to consider regarding aspects and behaviors of God. It has also shown that key information can often be located by finding and correcting words that have been mistranslated or that can be translated in different ways. It is hoped that, for you, it will be just the beginning of locating many "aha" moments, even for those who think they know the Bible well. This volume has not been intended to offer definitive answers to correct and expand understandings about the nature of God. Rather, its purpose has been to present multiple opportunities to consider alternate possibilities for the meanings of biblical texts, thereby guiding us to learn aspects and behaviors we may not have considered until now about God, in ways that God may be known and understood through the Bible. The systems of study presented here have also been intended to open new windows for research and understanding of the intended meanings of biblical narratives, and to offer a wider range of possibilities that present us with much to consider as we study and as we grow in our understanding of the Bible and in our knowledge of the nature and behavior of God!

APPENDIX

Study Resources

A PLAN OF ACTION FOR FURTHER BIBLICAL STUDY

In this addendum, some suggestions for a basic system will be spelled out for seeking various translations and finding alternate meanings to specific biblical texts. Employing such a system, or creating your own version of it, will assist you in getting on your own course of what can become a personal or group study regimen to help you grow in your study and in your faith life. The first plan offered will be for those who know some Hebrew and Greek. And an alternate plan will follow for those who do not yet know any Hebrew. Everyone learns differently. These study plans are only offered as outlines. As you read more and move forward and grow in your own scholarship, you will have no trouble filling in the blanks.

If you know some Hebrew and are a pastor or scholar with a library of academic books, your study plan might look something like this. (If you are a biblical scholar or theological or pastoral professional, you will already know this. Offered below is a list of suggestions or reminders!)

Gather the following books or similar/related books: Bibles with various translations, commentaries, Bible dictionaries, lexicons, concordances.

(The books listed below are only suggestions. If you don't own these, these or similar volumes will be available in theological libraries or online.)

BDB—*The Brown-Driver-Briggs Hebrew and English Lexicon* by Francis Brown, S. R. Driver, and Charles A. Briggs (Cambridge: Houghton, Mifflin, and Company, 1906; repr., Peabody, MA: Hendrickson 2010)—https://www.sefaria.org, https://hebrewcollege.edu, and https://www.blueletterbible.org.

TDOT—Theological Dictionary of the Old Testament edited by G. J. Botterweck, Helmer Ringren, and Heinz-Josef Fabry, trans. John T. Willis (Grand Rapids, MI: Eerdmans, 1974–2021)—https://www.logos.com and www.accordancebible.com.

LXX—*The Septuagint Version: Greek and English* by Sir Lancelot C. L. Brenton (Grand Rapids, MI: Zondervan, 1970)—https://www.septuagint.bible.

Concordance to the Septuagint: And the Other Greek Versions of the Old Testament (Including the Apocryphal Books) by Edwin Hatch and Henry A. Redpath (Graz, Austria: Ackademische Druk U, Verlagsansalt, 1897; repr., Grand Rapids, MI: Baker, 1987).

Dictionary of the Targumim, Talmud Babli, and Yerushalmi, and the Midrashic Literature, compiled by Marcus Jastrow (online as LaHaV's Jastrow Dictionary)—https://www.lahavlearning.com.

Interlinear Bible: OT, 2nd ed., edited by Jay P. Green Sr., 3 vols. (Peabody, MA: Hendrickson, 1985)—https://www.biblestudytools.com.

The Talmud: The Steinsaltz Edition; A Reference Guide by Adin Steinsaltz (New York: Random House, 1989)—https://steinsaltz-center.org/portal/library/Talmud.

JPS Hebrew English Tanakh by The Jewish Publication Society of America, Jan. 1, 2000—available online at http://jpsj.jps.jp.

The Five Books of Moses, translated by Everett Fox (New York: Schocken Books, 1997)—https://www.sefaria.org.

The Early Prophets: Joshua, Judges, Samuel and Kings, a New Translation with Introductions, Commentary, and Notes, by Everett Fox (New York: Schocken Books, 2014)—https://www.sefaria.org.

The Torah: A Modern Commentary, rev. ed., by Gunther Plaut and David E. S. Stein, eds. (New York: Union for Reform Judaism Press, 2006).

The Study Plan

1. Choose a passage from the Hebrew Bible / Old Testament, in English translation, that you wish to study, preferably one that contains a passage that has concerned you and that you want to know more about. Or, of course, it may be a passage from the lectionary on which you will be preaching or teaching in coming days or weeks.
2. Gather various English translations of the text you have chosen (e.g., NRSV, NIV, NKJV). This can also be done online with *Bible Hub* (https://biblehub.com) or *Bible Gateway* (https://biblegateway.com). (These are online Bible study suites. Bible Hub features classical Hebrew and *koine* Greek text analysis of any passage you choose in the various translations. This can be quick and useful for comparison of versions.)
3. Read the original text and then write out in Hebrew the passage(s) to be studied. Take note of particular words that have different translations into English.
4. Look up the Hebrew word(s) in a lexicon. How are they translated there? How many ways?
5. Look up the same text in the LXX. How would you translate the related Greek words directly into English? Are they the same English words found in the English-language biblical texts? If not, how do they differ? Which do you believe to be the most accurate translation? Why? Always take into

consideration the context of the passage with which you are working. Keep in mind that those who translated the text from the original Hebrew were so much closer in time to those who translated our Bibles into English. This does not necessarily make their translation more accurate. They could just as easily have misunderstood the meaning of the Hebrew word as we have. Still, there is also a chance theirs is more accurate.

6. Do the alternate translations present a different message, a radically different message, or the same message as the translation you have been trusting up until now? Which do you think might be the most accurate translation? Might they both be right?
7. Think about how you might prepare a sermon or a Bible study class on this passage. When you do present this, if possible, open for questions and take note of people's responses and insights.
8. Does an alternate translation or do people's responses change your attitudes about what the passage means or about God in any way? How did your new translation possibilities change you?

If you do not know any Hebrew, here is an alternate study plan. Choose a passage you have been curious about or about which you've been asked to speak.

1. Gather as many different copies of the Bible in English translation as you have access to. The different versions of a given passage can also be viewed online at *Bible Hub* or *Bible Gateway*.
2. Open each to the passage you want to study.
3. Take note of specific words in this passage that are of special interest to you.
4. Are there many different words in different English translations of your passage that express one thing? How

much alike or different are these words in the various translations? Do the words the translators have chosen fit appropriately with the rest of the sentence? The passage? Which translation seems likely to be the most accurate to you? Why? Do you think that your choice of translation is the most correct, or is it the one that most closely fits an agenda you already had before you began to study? Could they both be right?

5. Look at what is said about this passage in reliable commentaries and about these words in Bible dictionaries. See where the words or phrases are used in other passages of scripture.

Here are a few tips to remember when choosing which commentaries to read.

a. Always check the first couple of pages to learn what company published this book. Religious publishers tend toward or are directly connected to a religious denomination or, at least, come with specific denominational leanings. It is good, if you are able, to discern this. (Just as a very general example, Zondervan Christian Publishing tends to lean more in the conservative direction, and Pilgrim Press in the liberal.) All the publishers will stretch their limits to some extent, especially to publish a really good book. Still, it is wise to keep in mind that the various publishers do have agendas. It is good to intentionally read commentaries from a variety of directions if you keep in mind the possible mindsets from which they may emanate.
b. It is always important to take note of the footnotes and endnotes. Often, the most valuable information is hidden there in plain sight. Just as an example, sometimes a Bible footnote will say something like "This phrase/verse is absent in many early manuscripts." This could

indicate that the phrase or verse may have been added to the Bible much later than the rest of the material, although this is not necessarily the case. Alternately, sometimes a footnote will note that "many versions say . . . ," offering a different word, phrase, or sentence.

c. With commentaries and such, it is generally a good idea to take note of who wrote the commentary material that you are reading. The name of the author is usually listed. Do an internet search for that person. Find out their credentials and possibly also what you can learn about that person's denominational agenda.[1]

6. Always use your common sense. Keep in mind that you may be unknowingly desiring to find something to be what you wanted it to be. And, of course, that simply might not be the case. Still, always keep your idealism alive. After all, this work you are doing is all about God.

Employing Online Resources

Whether you are a biblical scholar, a pastor, a churchgoer, or just a person with curiosity about the Bible, you are living in a good time for gathering information! There are excellent digital resources available to make your work easier, such as *Logos* (https://www.logos.com) and *Accordance* (https://www.accordancebible.com).

Logos is available by subscription and offers instant access to a theological library of commentaries and other scholarly resources. It provides a choice of levels of subscription. The most advanced level includes original language tools.

Accordance Bible Software contains a library of thousands of volumes. It allows the user to run a search, look up definitions, view a

1 This statement is not intended to suggest that any one denomination is better or worse than any other. Still, all writers, intentionally or unintentionally, possess unacknowledged religious biases that may be reflected in their writings, and it is good to take this into consideration.

map, see a timeline, parse a word, hear a pronunciation or, of course, examine a chosen Bible passage.

Other digital programs available include *Olive Tree Bible Software,*[2] *theWord,*[3] *Bible Hub*, and *Bible Odyssey. Bible Hub* provides free online access to older Bible study tools including a Bible atlas, dictionaries, concordances, and the BDB. *Bible Odyssey* is a website supported by the Society of Biblical Literature and offers articles by scholars, a Bible dictionary, timelines, and maps.

There are situations in which the searcher may find very accurate Biblical information by simply looking the information up on *Google*. The danger in such a case is, of course, that the material gleaned may or may not be accurate. So the key to this is to be sure you know and trust the provider of that information if you are planning to use it in anything you are writing or preaching.

There is little doubt that the use of internet resources will increase in coming years. At the same time, at least partly due to the increase in use of AI, those of us who engage in research will have to be more and more careful about what material we choose to employ. This is especially true in matters related to our Bible and our God. The positive side to this digital resource issue is that hundreds of hours of labor are saved, and we do not have to live near major libraries and search through heavy books seeking out information that now is available to us at a touch of a finger. There is much for which to be thankful in living in these complex times.

A FEW WORDS ABOUT LEARNING BIBLICAL LANGUAGES

Yes, I am sure we agree that it would be a good thing if we could all study Biblical Hebrew and Greek. But there are many reasons why, both inside and outside of seminaries, this is happening less and less. Individuals, even those who desire greatly to study the Bible and

2 https://olivetree.com.

3 https://www.theword.net.

who wish to become faith leaders in the church, too often believe their study and work responsibilities are too great, and they simply cannot find the time required to learn the biblical languages. Others secretly fear that learning these languages would be too difficult and time-consuming, and they believe they can depend on the many translations to which we already have access.

All this said, there are manifold excellent reasons to study biblical languages. To know a language, even at a preliminary level, helps us to get closer to understanding the culture connected to it and to perceive the ways those who spoke that language saw their world. An individual word that is important to a people is often a word that requires many words to explain in another language! Knowing these words in the original language offers us a window into the ways of thinking of the people who used that language—in this case those people who wrote the biblical texts.

Learning Biblical Hebrew is not impossible. But it requires a plan for where to start and some understanding of how you will go about this study. It is not even possible, for example, to use a Hebrew dictionary until you have carefully learned the Hebrew alphabet and its order. You will also have to know that Hebrew is written and read from right to left. (This issue is not really a problem.) Once the letters are memorized and you can write them out, then you will be able to begin understanding how the language works, looking up words in a Hebrew dictionary, and memorizing vocabulary. Then, when you acquire and start to study with a teacher and have obtained a good Hebrew language textbook, you will be on your way. Once you get the basics under your belt, it is a very good idea to get into the habit of reading and translating portions of scripture every day. Even if you only do this for fifteen or twenty minutes a day, your language skills will grow. It is also good to continue increasing your Hebrew vocabulary. Some choose to make a flash card for each new word with English on one side and Hebrew or Greek on the other. It is then easy to go over these cards every day to keep them in your mind. It can also be great for Christians and scholars to attend synagogue worship services. The hymn and prayer books in many synagogues have Hebrew printed on one side of the page and English on the other. In time, you should be able to participate. Doing this also brings the Hebrew language to life in new ways. Be sure to check on the worship times as they will not be Sunday mornings.

For Biblical Greek, it is not much different. *Koine* Greek also has its own alphabet, which needs to be memorized at the outset. But Greek, like English, is read from left to right on the page.

The Greek language is easier than Hebrew for some. Hebrew seems easier to others. But one thing can be promised. And that is that the study of the biblical languages is always fulfilling and well worth any effort you choose to put into it.

In years past, most seminaries required both Biblical Hebrew and Biblical (*koine*) Greek languages be learned at the outset before any other classes even began. And it was required to complete these courses of study for graduation with a master of divinity degree or a PhD. PhD programs in biblical studies may also have required Aramaic in addition, as there is some Aramaic in the Bible.[4] Theology programs may have required Latin to be included because of the church's early use of the Vulgate.[5] Unfortunately, today, these languages still are taught, but too many seminaries have cut down to requiring only Greek, a choice of Hebrew or Greek as electives, or even no languages at all. In addition, many seminaries require the study of German and French, so the person will be able to access scholarship written in these languages.

There are, of course, extenuating circumstances for which a person might be granted an excuse from learning biblical languages, but, in this writer's opinion, this ought not be the norm. Some people are greatly burdened with time-consuming jobs and families to

---

4 Aramaic is found in the Hebrew Bible books of Ezra, Daniel, Jeremiah, and Genesis. Also, in the New Testament, Jesus speaks the Aramaic phrase *Talitha cumi*, which means "Little girl, arise," at Mark 5:41.

5 The Vulgate is a Latin translation of the Bible, which was compiled 383–404 CE by Saint Jerome.

support while they attend seminary. Some deal with wider cultural gaps. Those with more challenges ought also to have the opportunity to study scripture and enter the religious workforce. Still, everyone who is at all able will benefit beyond measure by studying the biblical languages!

Martin Luther (1483–1546) said that "we will not long preserve the gospel without the languages . . . the sheath in which the sword of the Spirit is contained." Luther viewed the biblical languages as a gift from God, essential for preserving the gospel and accurately teaching the Bible. He directly attributed his confidence and boldness at the time of the Reformation to a clear knowledge of scripture brought through understanding the original languages. And he was convinced that without the original languages, the gospel itself would be lost due to lack of clarity. Luther himself translated the Bible into German so the people would have access to the Word of God. Still, he understood and made it clear that the original languages had to be studied by those who would lead and others who were able. He wrote, "It is a sin and a shame not to know our own book or to understand the speech and words of our God. It is still a greater sin and loss that we do not study languages, especially in these days when God is offering and giving us people and books and every facility and inducement to this study and desires his Bible to be an open book. Oh, how happy the dear fathers would have been if they had our opportunity to study the languages and come thus prepared to the Holy Scriptures! What great toil and effort it cost them to gather up a few crumbs, while we with half the labor . . . can acquire the whole loaf."[6]

In the larger scheme of things (and in this world with all its changing dynamics), it may appear that other courses are more urgent than those that teach biblical languages. It is hoped that the examples that have been offered in this volume will show that

---

6 Martin Luther, "To the Councilmen of All Cities in Germany That They Establish and Maintain Christian Schools," a letter written by Luther in 1520. See Matthew Gilbert, "95 Quotes from Martin Luther," Oct 31, 2013, https://matgilbert.wordpress.com.

this is not at all the case and that, in fact, understanding the real meaning of the texts of scripture is vital, especially for those who will be our religious leaders and future teachers. The closer we can come to truly understanding the message of the Bible, the better will be our chances of helping build better lives for ourselves and those we love, better relationships, a better society, a stronger church, and a safer world.

Bibliography

Ackerman, Susan. *Gods, Goddesses, and the Women Who Serve Them.* Grand Rapids, MI: Eerdmans, 2022.

Albright, William F. "The Names Shaddai and Abram." *JBL* 54, no. 4 (1935): 180–93. https://doi.org/stable/3259784.

Alter, Robert. *The Art of Bible Translation.* Princeton, NJ: Princeton University Press, 2019.

———. *The Art of Biblical Poetry.* rev. ed. New York: Basic Books, 2011.

———. *The Hebrew Bible: A Translation with Commentary.* New York: W. W. Norton & Company, 2018.

Baljon, J. M. S. "Qur'anic Anthropomorphisms." *Islamic Studies* 27, no. 2 (1988): 119–27. https://www.jstor.org/stable/20839882.

Bergmann, Claudia D. "Mothers of a Nation: How Motherhood and Religion Intermingle in the Hebrew Bible." *Open Theology* 6, no. 1 (2020): 132–44. https://doi.org/10.1515/opth-2020-0012.

Biale, David. "The God with Breasts: El Shaddai in the Bible." *History of Religions* 21, no. 3 (1982): 240–56. https://www.jstor.org/stable/1062160.

Bloch, Ernst. *The Principle of Hope.* Translated by Neville Plaice and Paul Knight, 3 vols. Cambridge, MA: MIT Press, 1986. https://doi.org/2307/2505540.

Botterweck, G. J., Helmer Ringren, and Heinz-Josef Fabry, ed. *TDOT.* Translated by John T. Willis. Grand Rapids, MI: Eerdmans, 1974–2021.

Brown, Francis, S. R. Driver, and Charles A. Briggs, *Hebrew and English Lexicon of the Old Testament.* Oxford: Clarendon Press.

Brown, Francis, S. R. Driver, and Charles A. Briggs, *The New Brown - Driver - Briggs - Gesenius Hebrew English Lexicon*, Peabody, Massachusetts: Hendrickson.

Brueggemann, Walter. *Theology of the Old Testament: Testimony, Dispute, Advocacy.* Minneapolis: Fortress Press, 1997.

Budin, Stephanie Lynn. "Phallic Fertility in the Ancient Near East and Egypt, from part one of Inventing Generation." In *Reproduction: From Antiquity to the Present Day.* Edited by Nick Hopwood, Rebecca Flemming, and Lauren Kassell. Cambridge University Press, 2018. https://doi.org/10.1017/9781107705647.006.

Charbonnier, Edmond LaB. "In Defence of Anthropomorphism." In *Reflections on Mormonism: Judaeo-Christian Parallels*, edited by Truman G. Madsen, 433–437, Provo, UT: Brigham Young University, 1980. https://www.jstor.org/stable/44000643.

Clines, David J. A. "Alleged Female Language about the Deity in the Hebrew Bible." *JBL* 140, no. 2 (2021): 229–249. doi:10.1353/jbl2021.0011.

———, ed. *Concise Dictionary of Classical Hebrew*. Sheffield, UK: Sheffield Phoenix Press, 2009.

———. "The Most High Male: Divine Masculinity in the Bible." Paper delivered at the Feminist Interpretations section of the Society of Biblical Literature International Meeting, Buenos Aires, Argentina, July 22, 2015. www.academia.edu/14079928.

Cohen, Martin S. *The Shi'ur Qomah: Liturgy and Thiurgy in Pre-Kabbalistic Jewish Mysticism*. Lanham, MD: University Press of America, 1983.

Curtis, John Briggs. "On Job's Response to Yahweh." *JBL* 98, no. 4 (1979): 503. https://doi.org/10.2307/3265665.

Daly, Mary. *Beyond God the Father: Toward a Philosophy of Women's Liberation*. Eastbourne, UK: Gardner's Books, 1986.

Delitzsch, Friedrich. *Prolegomena eines neuen hebräisch-arämaischen Wörterbuchs zum Alten Testament*. Leipzig: J. C. Hinrichs'sche Buchhandlung, 1886.

———. *Assyrisches Handworterbuch*. Leipzig: J. C. Hinrichs'sche Buchhandlung, 1896).

Deutschmann, Barbara. *Creating Gender in the Garden: The Inconstant Partnership of Eve and Adam*. Library of Hebrew Bible/Old Testament Studies 729. New York: T&T Clark, 2022.

Dewey, David. A User's Guide to Bible Translations: Making the Most of Different Versions. Downers Grove, IL: InterVarsity Press, 2004.

Dombrowski, Daniel A. "Does God Have a Body?" *Journal of Speculative Philosophy*, n.s., 2, no. 3 (1988): 225–32.

Domoney-Lyttle, Zanne, and Sarah Nicholson, ed. *Women and Gender in the Bible: Texts, Intersections, Intertexts, Women and Gender in the Bible. Bible in the Modern World* 77, ed. Meredith J. C. Warren. Sheffield, UK: Sheffield Phoenix Press, 2021.

Edelman, Diana Vikander. ed. *The Triumph of Elohim: From Yahwisms to Judaisms*. Grand Rapids, MI: Eerdmans, 1995.

Eilberg-Schwartz, Howard. *God's Phallus and Other Problems for Men and Monotheism*. Boston: Beacon Press, 1995.

Emerton, J. A. "Yahweh and His Asherah: The Goddess or Her Symbols?" *Vetus Testamentum* 49, no. 3 (1999): 315–37. https://doi.org/10.1163/156853399774228010.

Erickson, Amy. "Without My Flesh I Will See God: Job's Rhetoric of the Body." *JBL* 132, no. 2 (2019): 295–313. https://doi.10.1353/jbl.2013.0034.

Fox, Everett. *The Early Prophets: Joshua, Judges, Samuel and Kings, a New Translation with Introductions, Commentary, and Notes*. New York: Schocken Books, 2014.

———, trans. *The Five Books of Moses: Genesis, Exodus, Leviticus, Numbers, Deuteronomy; A New Translation with Introductions, Commentary, and*

Notes by Everett Fox. Vol. 1 of The Schocken Bible. New York: Schocken Books, 1983.

Frankfort, Henri. *Kingship and the Gods: A Study of Near Eastern Religion as the Integration of Society and Nature*. 1948. Reprint, Chicago: University of Chicago Press, 1978.

Frevel, Christian. *History of Ancient Israel*. Atlanta: SBL Press, 2023, https://doi.org/10.2307/JJ4470334.3.

Frymer-Kensky, Tikva. *In the Wake of the Goddess: Women, Culture, and the Biblical Transformation of Pagan Myth*. New York: Fawcett Columbine, 1992.

———. *Motherprayer: A Pregnant Woman's Spiritual Companion*. New York: Riverhead, 1996.

Gottstein, Alon Goshen. "The Body as Image of God in Rabbinic Literature." *Harvard Theological Review* 87, no. 2 (1994): 171–95, https://doi.org/10.1017/50017816000032776.

Granerod, Gard. "A Forgotten Reference to Divine Procreation? Psalm 2:6 in the Light of Egyptian Royal Ideology." *Vetus Testamentum* 60, no. 3 (2010): 323–36. https://doi.10.1163/156853310X498980.

Grossman, Jonathan. "Ambiguity in the Biblical Narrative and Its Contribution to the Literary Formation." PhD diss., Bar Ilan University, 2006. https://orcid.org/0000-0003-2072-6194.

Gruber, Yeshaya. "Creative and Destructive Work: Greek and Slavic Distributaries of Hebrew and Biblical Lifeblood." In *Furthering Interfaith Biblical Scholarship: A Festschrift in Memory of André LaCocque*, edited by Doreen M. McFarlane. Eugene, OR: Pickwick, 2024.

Gudbergsen, Thomas. "God Consists of Both the Male and the Female Genders: A Short Note on Gen 1:27." *Vetus Testamentum* 62, no. 3 (2012): 450–52. https://www.jstor.org/stable/41583767.

Gunkel, Hermann. *Einleitung in die Psalmen*. 1933. Reprint, Gottingen, Germany: Vandenhoeck & Ruprecht, 1985.

Habel, Norman C. *The Book of Job: A Commentary*. Old Testament Library. Philadelphia: Westminster Press, 1985.

Haines, Alastair. "The Masculine Language of the Bible: A Response to David Clines." *New Male Studies: An International Journal* 5, no. 1 (2016): 5–30. https://www.academia.edu/20633158/The_masculine_language_of_the_Bible_A_response_to_David_Clines.

Hadromi-Allouche, Zohar, Nirmal Fernando, and Keren Abbou Hershkovitz, ed. *Scriptural Sexualities*. Publication forthcoming.

Hart, David Bentley, trans. *The New Testament: A Translation*. New Haven, CT: Yale University Press, 2017.

Hatch, Edwin, and Henry A. Redpath. *Concordance to the Septuagint and the Other Greek Versions of the Old Testament (Including the Apocryphal Books)*. Graz, Austria: Akademische Druck.U. Verlagsanstalt, 1954. Reprint, Grand Rapids, MI: Baker, 1998.

Heinemann, Joseph. "The Status of the Labourer in Jewish Law and Society in the Tannaitic Period." *Hebrew Union College Annual* 25 (1954): 263–325. https://www.jstor.org/stable/i23502447.

Hoffmeier, James K. "The Arm of God vs the Arm of Pharoah in the Exodus Narratives." *Biblica* 67, no. 3 (1986): 378–87. https://www.jstor.org/stable/42611033.

Hornblower, G. D. "Osiris and the Fertility Rite." *Man* 41, no. 71 (1941): 94–103, https://doi.org/10.2307/2792421.Jastrow, Marcus, comp. *A Dictionary of the Targamim, the Talmud Babli, and Yerushalmi, and the Midrashic Literature.* Vol. 1. New York: Judaica Press, 1992.

Kanarek, Jane. "The Warrior God as Midwife." *Sh'ma: A Journal of Jewish Responsibility.* April 1, 2011, 3–4. http://shma.com.

Keel, Othmar, and Christoph Uehlinger. *Gods, Goddesses, and Images of Ancient Israel.* Minneapolis: Fortress Press, 1998.

Kerenyi, Carl. *Archetypical Image of Indestructible Life.* Princeton, NJ: Princeton University Press, 1976.

Kirova, Milena. *Performing Masculinity in the Hebrew Bible.* Hebrew Bible Monographs 91. Sheffield, UK: Sheffield Phoenix Press, 2020.

LaCocque, André. *Esther Regina: A Bakhtinian Reading.* Rethinking Theory. Evanston, IL: Northwestern University Press, 2008.

———. *The Feminine Unconventional: Four Subversive Figures in Israel's Tradition.* Minneapolis: Fortress Press, 1990. Reprint, Eugene, OR: Wipf and Stock, 2005.

———. *Work and Creativity: A Philosophical Study from Creation to Post-Modernity.* New York: Lexington, 2020.

Lapinkivi, Pirjo. "The Sumerian Sacred Marriage and Its Aftermath in Later Sources." In *Sacred Marriages: The Divine-Human Sexual Metaphor from Sumer to Early Christianity.* Edited by Martti Nissinen and Risto Uro. Ann Arbor, MI: Eisenbrauns, 2008. https://doi.org/10.5325/j.ctv1bxgzv8.4.

Leslie, Elmer A. *The Psalms.* New York: Abingdon-Cokesbury Press, 1949.

Levinson, Hanne Loland. "Still Invisible after All These Years? Female God-Language in the Hebrew Bible: A Response to David J. A. Clines." *JBL 141*, no. 2 (2022). https://doi.org10.15699/jbl.1412.2022.1.

Lipka, Hilary, and Bruce Wells, ed. *Sexuality and the Law in the Torah. Library of Hebrew Bible/Old Testament Studies* 675. London: T&T Clark, 2020.

Maier, Christl M. *Daughter Zion, Mother Zion: Gender, Space, and the Sacred in Ancient Israel.* Minneapolis: Fortress Press, 2008.

Marcus, Yosef, comp., *Pirkei Avot: Ethics of the Fathers.* Brooklyn: Kehot Publication Society, 2009.

Markschies, Christoph. *God's Body: Jewish, Christian, and Pagan Images of God.* Translated by Alexander Johannes Edmonds. Waco, TX: Baylor University Press, 2019.

McFague, Sallie. *Metaphorical Theology: Models of God in Religious Language.* Philadelphia: Fortress Press, 1982.

McFarlane, Doreen M. "How Biblical Translation Choices Forward Clergy Power and Control." Lecture delivered at the Bible in America section of the Society of Biblical Literature Annual Meeting, San Diego, CA, November 25, 2024.

———."Wedded to Power: Two Biblical Women Married to Kings." In *Furthering Interfaith Biblical Scholarship: A Festschrift in Memory of André LaCocque*, edited by Doreen M. McFarlane. Eugene, OR: Pickwick, June 2025, 130–139.

———. "Lost in Translation: The Sexuality of God in Hebrew Scripture, the New Testament, and the Qur'an." Paper presented at the Society of Biblical Literature International Meeting, Salzburg, Austria, July 22, 2022.

———. "Lost in Translation: Gender and Sexuality of God in the Hebrew Bible." In *Scriptural Sexualities*, edited by Zohar Hadromi-Allouche, Nirmal Fernando, and Keren Abbou Hershkovitz. Publication forthcoming.

Meshel, Naphtali. "Whose Job Is This? Dramatic Irony and Double-Entendre in the Book of Job." In *The Book of Job: Aesthetics and Hermeneutics*, edited by Leora Batnitzky and Hana Pardes. Berlin: de Gruyter, 2014. https://doi.org/10.1515/9783110338799.47.

Meyers, Alicia D. "In the Father's Bosom: Breastfeeding and Identity Formation in John's Gospel." *Catholic Biblical Quarterly* 76, no. 3 (2014): 481–442. https://www.jstor.org/stable/43728353.

Moder, Ally. "Woman, Personhood, and the Male God: A Feminist Critique of Patriarchal Concepts of God in View of Domestic Abuse." *Feminist Theology* 28, no. 1 (2019): 85–103. https://doi.org/10.1177/0966735019859471.

Moore Cross, Frank. *Canaanite Myth and Hebrew Epic: Essays in the History of the Religion of Israel.* 1973. Reprint, Cambridge, MA: Harvard University Press, 1997.

Neusner, Jacob. *Normative Judaism.* Vol. 1 of *Origins of Judaism.* New York: Garland, 1990.

Nissinen, M., and F. Stavrakopolou. "Introductions: New Perspectives on Body and Religion." *Hebrew Bible and Ancient Israel* 2, no. 3 (2013): 453–57. https://doi.org/10.1628/219222713X13933396528243.

Peleg, Yitzik. "Two Readings: Sexual Verbs and Ambiguity in the Biblical Story." In *Scriptural Sexualities*, edited by Zohar Hadromi-Allouche, Nirmal Fernando, and Keren Abbou Hershkovitz. Publication forthcoming.

Plaut, Gunther, and David E. S. Stein. *The Torah: A Modern Commentary.* rev. ed., New York: Union for Reform Judaism Press, 2006.

Pomeroy, Sarah B. *Goddesses, Whores, Wives, and Slaves: Women in Classical Antiquity.* New York: Schocken Books, 1975.

Pope, Marvin. *Book of Job.* Anchor Bible Commentaries. Garden City, New York: Doubleday, 1965.

Rouhier-Willoughby, Jeanmarie. "Birth Customs: Ancient Traditions in Modern Guise." *The Slavic and Eastern European Journal* 47, no. 2 (2003): 227–50. https://doi.org/10.2307/3219945.

Seo, Bo-Myung. "The Dialectic of Praxis and the Theology of Work." In *Furthering Interfaith Biblical Scholarship: A Festschrift in Memory of André LaCocque*, edited by Doreen M. McFarlane. Eugene, OR: Pickwick, 2024.

Somner, Benjamin D. *The Bodies of God and the World of Ancient Israel.* Cambridge: Cambridge University Press, 2009.

Soskice, Janet Martin. *Metaphor and Religious Language.* Oxford: Clarendon Press, 1985.

Stavrakopoulou, Francesca. *God: An Anatomy.* New York: Alfred A. Knopf, January 2022.

Stead, Christopher. *Philosophy in Christian Antiquity.* Cambridge: Cambridge University Press, 1994.

Steinsaltz, Adin. *The Talmud: The Steinsaltz Edition; A Reference Guide.* New York: Random House, 1989.

Tiemeyer, Lena-Sophia. "The Lover and the Friend: The Depiction of Jonathan's Sexuality in Contemporary Literature." In *Scriptural Sexualities*, edited by Zohar Hadromi-Allouche, Nirmal Fernando, and Keren Abbou Hershkovitz. Publication forthcoming.

Vermeulen, Karolien, and Elizabeth R. Hayes. *How We Read the Bible: A Guide to Scripture's Style and Meaning.* Grand Rapids, MI: Eerdmans, 2022.

von Rad, Gerhard. *Old Testament Theology.* New York: HarperCollins, 1962.

Wagner, Andreas. *God's Body: The Anthropomorphic God in the Old Testament.* Translated by Marion Salzmann. London: T&T Clark, 2019.

Weipert, Manfred. "Erwagungen zur Etymologie des Gottesnamens 'El Shaddai.'" *Zeitschrift der Deutschen Morgenlandischen Gesellschaft* 111, no. 36 (1961): 42–62.

Williams, Wesley. "A Body Unlike Bodies: Transcendent Anthropomorphism in Ancient Semitic Tradition and Early Islam." *Journal of the American Oriental Society* 129, no. 1 (2009). 19–44. https://doi.org/10.2307/40593866.

Index

Abbreviations, xi
Abraham and Sarah, 21
Ackerman, Susan, 91
Adam, 16–17
Advocate, 19
Afterlife, 84
Albright, William F., 94
Alter, Robert, 71, 94, 99, 143
Apostles' Creed, 84
Aramaic, 155
Arguing with God, 29
Arm of God, 87–90
Asherah, consort of Yahweh, 90–91
Authorship, biblical, 8

Ba'al, the god, 89
Bathsheba, 22
Bentley, David Hart, 11
Bergmann, Claudia D., 97, 107
Bezalmenu – in our image, 17
Biale, David, 93
Bibliography, 159–164
Brueggemann, Walter, 135
Budin, Stephanie Lynn, 89
Burning Bush, 95

Canaanites, 57
Clementine Vulgate, 5
Clines, David J. A., 91–92, 100–103
Co-creators, 116
Commentaries, choosing, 151–152
Copying texts, 10
Creation, 133–139
Creation narratives, 16
Creation only God can do – *bara*, 133–136
Curtis, John Briggs, 33
Cyrus, 56

David, 22, 45
Dead Sea Scrolls, 7
Death, 73
Dedication, 5
Delitsch, Friedrich, 94
Demutemu -according to our likeness, 17
Deus absconditus – hidden God, 127–128
Deutschmann, Barbara, 18
Dewey, David, 6, 7, 8
Dionysus, 89
Disagreement, 29–41

Eating the fruit, 20
Edomites, 56
Elberg-Schwartz, Howard, 93
Elijah, 38–39, 41, 80
Elisha, 80
El Shaddai as a fertility blessing, 93, 97
Embodiment, 85–107
Emerton, J. A., 91
Emotions, 109–113
Enemies, 51–60
Esther, 21, 23
Ex-nihilo, 73, 74–75

Ezekiel, 81
Ezer – advocate/help, 18–20
Ezer kenegdo – fitting companion, 18

Female genital mutilation, 27–28
Format, 12–13
Frevel, Christian, 57, 90
Frymer-Kensky, Tikva, 23, 24, 103

God Almighty, 94–97
God as *abba*, 126
God as husband, 62
God as male, 87–91
God as metaphor, 92–93
God as a midwife, 98, 99, 100–102
God as a mother, 102–103
God as other, 138–139
God as parent, 62
God as patriarchal, 104
God as repentant, 43–46
God as a rock, 97–98
God as spirit, 85
God as zealous/jealous, 109–111
God bargaining, 44
God birthing and begetting, 97–99
God, body of, 85–87
God, image of, 17
God, outstretched arm of, 87–90
God siring a king, 99
God unchanging, 49
God of wrath, 61, 68
God, names of, 123–131
God with breasts, 93, 95
God with a consort, 90–91
God with female attributes, 91–93
God with womb, 99–100
God's name to Moses, 95
Gods, Ugaritic, 89
Good News, 142–145
Gruber, Yeshaya, 117, 118, 121
Gutenberg Press, 10

Hagar, 21, 125
Haines, Alastair, 92
Hapax legomena, 11
Heinemann, Joseph, 119
Hierarchy, 15–28
Helper, Woman as, 18–20
Hermes, 89
Hierarchy, 15–28
Hinrichs, J.C., 94
Hoffmeier, James, 87, 88
Hornblower, G. D., 89
Humans as co-creators, 116
Hosea, 61

Isis and Horus, 96
Isis and Osiris, gods, 89

Jehovah, 127
Job, the man, 29–34, 135–136
Job's daughters, 32–33
Job's "friends", 30
Job's response to God, 31
Jonah, 52–56

Kanarek, Jane, 102
Kerenyi, Carl, 89
Kirkman, Mackenzie, 104

LGBTQIA+2S, 16
LaCocque, A., 20, 23, 87, 116, 119
Languages, biblical – about learning, 153–157
Latin, 155
Levinson, Hanne Loland, 92
Love in Hebrew scripture, 61–69
Loving-kindness, 65
Luther, Martin, on the importance of learning biblical languages, 156
Lydia, 24

Maier, Christl M., 93, 98
Male dominance, 21
Male – female relations, 16
Man, as obedient to woman, 20–21
Marx, Karl, 116
Matriarchal society, 87
Matriarchs, 80

McFague, Sallie, 92
McFarlane, Doreen M., 5, 21, 85–86
Mesha Stele, 127
Meshel, Naphtali, 32, 34
Messiah (Handel's oratorio), 80
Micah, 61
Min, the god, 89
Moabites, 56
Moore Cross, Frank, 89, 95, 99
Moses and the Golden Calf, 44
Mystery of Faith, 84

Naham, 52
Nephesh – soul/whole being, 71–72, 76
Niehr, Herbert, 90, 95
Ninevites, 53–56

Online resources, employing, 152–153
Oratorios, 7
Oswold, Debra L., 104

Patriarchal society, 24
Peleg, Yitzik, 144
Pharisees, 80
Pharaoh, 88
Philistines, 56
Pirkei Avot, 116
Poetry, Hebrew, 8–9

Queen of Heaven, 90–91

Rebirth, 80
Redeemer, 64
Repentance, 43–50
Resurrection, 79–84

Sadducees, 80
Sailors in Jonah, 53–56
Satan, 30–31, 60
Scribes, the work of, 10
Schuessler-Fiorenza, Elizabeth, 91
Scriptorium, 10
Seo, Bo-Myung, 116
Septuagint (LXX), 73
Shadu – mountain, 94
Sheol, 81
Simon, Howard, 104
Sin, 76
Sins of the world, 81
Solomon, 22
Soskice, Janet Martin, 93
Stavrakopolou, Francesca, 90, 96
Study Resources and Plan, with Hebrew, 147–150
Study Resources and Plan, without Hebrew, 150–152

Tiemeyer, Lena-Sophia, 105
Translations, 5–12, 13–14, 142–145
Translations, rhythm and flow of, 143
Trinity, 125
Troud, Slavic word for work, 117

Wagner, Andreas, 87, 88
War, 51–52
"Wedded to Power", 21
Weippert, Manfred, 94
Wholeness, 71–77
Woman as advocate/help, 18–20, 27–28
Woman's beauty, 24
Woman's equality, 24
Woman's Power, 23
Women, subservience of, 16
Word, interpretation of, 11
Words with opposite meanings, 11
Work, 116–121
Work as *avodah*, 116
Work as a gift, 116
Work as *mitzvot*, 118
Work - Slavic meanings, 117
Work as Worship and Service, 115–121

Yahweh, YHWH, 95–97, 126–128

Zephaniah, 52
Zeus, 89